TERRORISM

Praise for books by Richard English:

Armed Struggle: The History of the IRA (2003)

Winner of the Political Studies Association Politics Book of the Year Award for 2003

'a work which eclipses all other studies of the IRA and must now be regarded as the single most important book on the topic...a penetrating and rewarding study' *Times Literary Supplement*

'an essential book...closely-reasoned, formidably intelligent and utterly compelling...required reading across the political spectrum...important and riveting' *The Times*

'an outstanding new book on the IRA...a calm, rational but in the end devastating deconstruction of the IRA' *Observer*

'superb...the first full history of the IRA and the best overall account of the organization...sets a new standard for debate on republicanism'

Irish Times

Irish Freedom: The History of Nationalism in Ireland (2006)

Winner of the Christopher Ewart-Biggs Memorial Prize for 2007
Winner of the Political Studies Association of Ireland Book Prize for 2007

'superb survey of Irish nationalism...fine work of scholarship...ambitious, epic work on Irish nationalism' *Observer*

'a brilliant one-volume history of Ireland...[a] formidable study'

Guardian

'Richard English has followed up his award-winning *Armed Struggle: The History of the IRA* with another survey of a vast topic: the past origins, past and present progress and future potential of that elusive and yet everyday phenomenon: national identity in Ireland...This is a very ambitious endeavour, and English brings it off with great panache...courageous and successful'

Irish Times

'a stimulating and learned study that deserves to be widely read'

New Statesman

TERRORISM
HOW TO RESPOND

RICHARD ENGLISH

OXFORD
UNIVERSITY PRESS

OXFORD

UNIVERSITY PRESS

Great Clarendon Street, Oxford OX2 6DP

Oxford University Press is a department of the University of Oxford.
It furthers the University's objective of excellence in research, scholarship,
and education by publishing worldwide in

Oxford New York

Auckland Cape Town Dar es Salaam Hong Kong Karachi
Kuala Lumpur Madrid Melbourne Mexico City Nairobi
New Delhi Shanghai Taipei Toronto

With offices in

Argentina Austria Brazil Chile Czech Republic France Greece
Guatemala Hungary Italy Japan Poland Portugal Singapore
South Korea Switzerland Thailand Turkey Ukraine Vietnam

Oxford is a registered trade mark of Oxford University Press
in the UK and in certain other countries

Published in the United States
by Oxford University Press Inc., New York

British Library Cataloguing in Publication Data

Data available

Library of Congress Cataloging in Publication Data

English, Richard.
Terrorism : how to respond / Richard English.
p. cm.
ISBN 978-0-19-922998-7
1. Terrorism. 2. Terrorism—Prevention. I. Title.
HV6431.E548 2009
363.325—dc22   2009009586

Typeset by SPI Publisher Services, Pondicherry, India
Printed in Great Britain
on acid-free paper by
Clays Ltd, St Ives plc

ISBN 978-0-19-922998-7

1 3 5 7 9 10 8 6 4 2

For Maxie

CONTENTS

PREFACE

We face two kinds of terrorist problem. One is practical, the other analytical, and our difficulties in responding to the former have been significantly exacerbated by our failings in regard to the latter.

The practical problem is well known, hugely important, and all too pressing. Terrorism, and our response to it, are among the most compelling of global political issues: they dominate news headlines, public anxiety, and political strategies alike across much of the contemporary world. In the long shadow of 9/11, Madrid, Bali, and 7/7 London, of the conflicts in Iraq and Afghanistan, and of violent tensions such as those in Israel/Palestine or Pakistan, terrorism and the appropriate responses to terrorism between them represent one of the most significant challenges for states and societies in the twenty-first century.

The analytical problem lies in the interconnected questions of definition, explanation, and history. What is terrorism? How best can we approach the task of explaining it? What lessons can we learn from our historical experience of it?

I think it's clear that these two problems—the practical and the analytical—are closely interwoven. It is true that no amount of analytical precision or insight will rid us of the existence of terrorism as an ongoing practical problem. But a central premiss of this book is that we could respond far more effectively than we do to the practical terrorist problem if only our analysis of definition, explanation, and history was sharper, more accurate, and more integrated. If we want to respond effectively to terrorism, then we need to learn carefully from historical experience; in order to do that, we must adopt the most appropriate way of explaining and understanding it; and such explanation and understanding can be developed only if we clearly, credibly, plausibly, and honestly define the phenomenon that we actually face.

So in this book I'll deal in sequence with links in a chain of concatenated argument. Chapter 1 will address the problem of definition and asks the question, 'What is Terrorism?' Chapter 2 focuses on the problem of explanation and attempts to address the question, 'Why do People Resort to Terror?' Chapter 3 examines the problem of history, asking 'What can we Learn from Terrorism Past?' And Chapter 4 concentrates on the problem of response: in practical terms, 'How Should We Respond?'

Such an interlinked argument could have been made effectively enough prior to the crisis prompted by the events of 11 September 2001. But the post-9/11 years have raised to higher levels the potential dangers of terrorism and of reactions to it, and the post-2001 response to terrorism has been both analytically and practically flawed in a very dangerous manner. Despite the extraordinary efforts and resources devoted to the twenty-first-century War on Terror, the reality is that terrorist attacks and threats have not diminished in the post-9/11 period. Indeed, some of the tactics adopted in order to try to suppress terrorism, have instead deepened that very disaffection from which terrorist atrocity is generated and by which it is sustained. Rather than achieving its intended aim of isolating and defeating a small band of terrorist zealots, the mixture of massive military deployment, hasty and often ineffective legal initiatives, and sometimes dubious practices of detention and prisoner treatment, has served instead to render the violent strategies of anti-Western terrorists more, rather than less, alluring to significant sections of the (in particular, Islamic) community across the globe. In all of this, a sharper and more integrated analysis regarding definition, explanation, history, and response could have helped greatly. I hope that such an analysis might also help us deal more effectively with the challenges to be faced now and, inevitably, in the future.

Terrorism: How to Respond is intended as a concise, accessible, scholarly, and practical contribution towards this further understanding. My primary aim is to stimulate productive debate on the subject as we necessarily rethink our complex responses to it. In particular, it seems to me important that those of us who studied terrorist violence in specific contexts for years prior to 9/11 should engage with the problems magnified, and to some extent altered, by the attacks of that day. I think it's vital that we all now learn from historical experience, and so I have tried here to set out some of the lessons drawn from the particular Irish case study with which I'm most familiar. I hope that this, along with my reflections on definition, explanation, and wider historical experience, will offer some valuable insight as we develop our necessary response to the terrorist problem.

ACKNOWLEDGEMENTS

I delivered numerous public lectures on terrorism while working on this book, and I particularly benefited from questions and comments offered by audiences at the following: the University of Chicago; the University of California, San Diego; the University of Oxford; the London School of Economics; the Catholic University of America in Washington, DC; the University of New Hampshire; San Diego State University; and Queen's University, Belfast. As ever with my research, I have been indebted to the staffs of numerous libraries and archives. I would especially like to thank those at the British Library (London), Queen's University (Belfast), and the Linen Hall Library (Belfast). My many interviewees over the years have been generous in taking the time to meet me, while colleagues and students at Queen's University, Belfast, once again provided an excellent environment within which to work. Bruce Hunter's advice was much appreciated throughout, as were the editorial enthusiasm and professionalism of Luciana O'Flaherty, Matthew Cotton, and their colleagues at Oxford University Press.

RE

Belfast, August 2008

LIST OF PLATES

LIST OF ABBREVIATIONS

CBRN	Chemical, Biological, Radiological, or Nuclear [weapons]
CIA	Central Intelligence Agency
DUP	Democratic Unionist Party
EOKA	Ethniki Organosis Kyprion Agoniston
ETA	Euskadi Ta Askatasuna
FBI	Federal Bureau of Investigation
FLN	Front de Libération Nationale
INLA	Irish National Liberation Army
IRA	Irish Republican Army
LHLPC	Linen Hall Library, Political Collection (Belfast)
LTTE	Liberation Tigers of Tamil Elam
PKK	Kurdistan Workers' Party
PLO	Palestine Liberation Organization
PNV	Partido Nacionalista Vasco
RAF	Red Army Faction
SDLP	Social Democratic and Labour Party
UDA	Ulster Defence Association
UFF	Ulster Freedom Fighters
UUP	Ulster Unionist Party
UVF	Ulster Volunteer Force
WMD	Weapons of Mass Destruction

1

WHAT IS TERRORISM?

It is the summer of 1999 in the garden of 10 Downing Street. Two middle-aged men are playing amicably with UK Prime Minister Tony Blair's children: they attempt to ride the skateboard belonging to one of these children along a path through the rose garden,[1] and the image appears serene and benign. In the early 1970s these two men—Martin McGuinness and Gerry Adams—had been leading figures within the Provisional Irish Republican Army,[2] and even during their skateboarding middle age they remained on the IRA's ruling Army Council.[3]

During the lengthy campaign presided over by that Army Council, of course, the IRA had not always been on such amiable terms with the inhabitant of 10 Downing Street. In October 1984 an IRA Semtex bomb came close to killing Prime Minister Margaret Thatcher; yet one of the perpetrators of that Brighton bombing, Patrick Magee, would dispute the claim that he or his republican comrades, McGuinness and Adams, should be described as 'terrorists' at all. Magee himself served fourteen years in prison for his part in the Brighton attack, but he considers the term 'terrorist' to be 'debased currency': as used by people such as President George W. Bush against America's enemies, the word 'terrorism' has—as Magee put it to me—been one 'more often applied tendentiously or pejoratively, not to explain or clarify but to obscure. "Terrorism" has become a non-explanation designed to perpetuate injustice, repression, and many gross asymmetries of power. As it's been said, a terrorist is the one with the little bomb.'[4]

These words and images clearly point to one of the most pressing and difficult issues of our time. We cannot adequately explain terrorism unless we are precise about what it is that we are seeking to explain. So I think we must begin by asking the crucial question: what is terrorism? For example, is the Brighton bomber at all justified in rejecting the term 'terrorism' when it is applied to violence such as his own? Is anti-state violence like that of the IRA any more terrorizing, or any less justified, than the far more lethal violence carried out in recent decades for political purposes by states against civilians? If Martin McGuinness and Gerry Adams deserved the term 'terrorist' during their 1970s IRA careers—and most people would probably think that they *did*—then were they, as IRA Army Council members, any less worthy of that description while they discussed peace with Tony Blair and played cosily with his children in the late 1990s? If *not*, then was the British state right, in fact, to talk to Irish terrorists in this manner, and what are the implications for international politics of our answer to that question?

These are complex issues, and they reflect the first problem that I want to try to solve in this book: namely, that of definition. This problem of terrorist definition is absolutely vital and, as is well known, it is also difficult and many-layered. Indeed, there are really many *problems* of definition, and it might be helpful to consider some of the more significant ones, before attempting to set out a working definition upon which this book and its argument can be based.

First, there is the difficulty that there exist so many competing definitions of terrorism that, as one expert has aptly put it, the phenomenon is 'shrouded in terminological confusion'.[5] The word 'terrorism' has been used in so many ways, to refer to so many different (though often partially overlapping) kinds of act, that it has become rather blurred in its usage. Even different wings of the same state have used definitions which are at odds with one another. The US State Department, for example, has defined terrorism as 'Premeditated, politically motivated violence perpetrated against noncombatant targets by subnational groups or clandestine agents, usually intended to influence an audience'.[6] But the US Federal Bureau of Investigation (FBI) defines it rather differently, as 'the use of serious violence against persons or property, or the threat to use such violence, to intimidate or coerce a government, the public, or any section of the public in order to promote political, social or ideological objectives'.[7] Yet again, the US Department of Defense in 1990 described terrorism as 'the unlawful use of, or threatened use of, force or violence against individuals or property to coerce and intimidate governments or societies, often to achieve political, religious or ideological objectives'.[8] The variations between these definitions (only 'perpetrated' violence, or violence used and/or *threatened*, for example) are significant enough to generate a measure of confusion and potentially unhelpful ambiguity.

Competing definitions at state level—and also between different states—are echoed in the plethora of dictionary and scholarly definitions of this seemingly protean term. Dictionaries can valuably alert us to key dimensions of the phenomenon. But we can see that they do so in a divergent manner, with terrorism involving 'an organized system of intimidation, esp. for political ends',[9] but alternatively a terrorist being 'a person who uses or favours violent and intimidating methods of coercing a government or community'.[10]

Scholarly definitions also vary in significant ways. Terrorism has been defined as 'the deliberate use of violence, or threat of its use, against innocent people, with the aim of intimidating them, or other people, into a course of action they otherwise would not take'.[11] But others have played down the role of threatened action, while specifying more narrowly the identity of the actor and the victim ('We define "terrorism" as the use of violence against civilians by non-state actors to attain political goals'[12]). Yet another useful formulation sees terrorism involving the tactic or policy of carrying out a 'political act, ordinarily committed by an organized group, which involves the intentional killing or other severe harming of non-combatants or the threat of the same or intentional severe damage to the property of non-combatants or the threat of the same'.[13] In contrast, Professor Conor Gearty's admirable desire for clarity introduces the features of random target selection and widespread broadcasting of a case: 'Violence is unequivocally terrorist when it is politically motivated and carried out by sub-state groups; when its victims are chosen at random; and when the purpose behind the violence is to communicate a message to a wider audience.'[14] Other dimensions can also be added, including that of acquiring followers: 'Terrorism involves the use of violence by an organization other than a national government to intimidate or frighten a target audience. In general, terrorism has two broad purposes: to gain supporters and to coerce opponents.'[15]

What are we to make of this wide range of different definitions? All of the above have been chosen because they are laudable, impressive attempts at precision and honest definition. But it is tempting to allow oneself slightly lengthier definitional space, in order to achieve yet greater accuracy. So one leading terrorism expert, Professor Bruce Hoffman, has helpfully argued that terrorism involves politically motivated violence or threatened violence, 'designed to have far-reaching psychological repercussions beyond the immediate victim or target', carried out by a sub-national or non-state, non-uniformed organization 'with an identifiable chain of command or conspiratorial cell structure'; terrorism, he continues, is

> the deliberate creation and exploitation of fear through violence or the threat of violence in the pursuit of political change. All terrorist acts involve violence or the threat of violence. Terrorism is specifically designed to have far-reaching psychological effects beyond the immediate victim(s) or object of the terrorist attack. It is meant to instil fear within, and thereby intimidate, a wider 'target audience' that might include a rival ethnic or religious group, an entire country, a national government or political party, or public opinion in general. Terrorism is designed to create power where there is none or to consolidate power where there is very little. Through the publicity generated by their violence, terrorists seek to obtain the leverage, influence, and power they otherwise lack to effect political change on either a local or an international scale.[16]

It's hardly surprising that there exist so many competing and varying definitions of terrorism, since the phenomenon has itself been so varied in context, form, and objective: for one thing, 'Terrorism is a *method* which can be used for an infinite variety of goals.'[17] Indeed, one central aspect of the terrorist problem is the reality that no single definition will prove *entirely* satisfactory in itself. As we'll see during the rest of this chapter, there are problems with even the valuable definitions cited already, and no author should be naïve enough to assume that they will produce a final, universally agreed definition of the 'T' word. But the existence of so many varying definitions arguably makes it more important still that anyone discussing terrorism should establish precisely what they themselves take the term to mean, and why.

In doing so, it's necessary to consider some other definitional problems. One concerns what might be termed the problem of literal terror. The word 'terrorism' is derived from the Latin 'terrere': to frighten, terrify, deter, or scare away. Terrorist violence can clearly involve all of this, and the phenomenon is often read as being crucially founded on such capacities: 'What makes an act terrorism is that it terrifies';[18] 'all uses of political violence effect some degree of fear', but in 'terrorism proper, the causing of fear and coercion through fear is *the* objective': 'Terrorism is meant to cause terror (extreme fear) and, when successful, does so.... Terrorism is intimidation with a purpose: the terror is meant to cause others to do things they would otherwise not do. Terrorism is coercive intimidation.'[19]

Certainly, in the wake of atrocities, there is understandable prominence given to the 'terror' involved in terrorism. After the 7/7 attacks in London in 2005, newspaper reports were full of 'shocked survivors' and of 'innocent people stunned by sudden horror'; eyewitnesses recorded that 'There was panic and everyone was running', told of people 'screaming and screaming', and reported that 'Some people descended into hysterical panic'. One of the 'terrified passengers' trapped on a bomb-attacked train recalled that 'There was a massive shudder and the train ground to a halt.... The explosion seemed to come from the next carriage to me. For a few seconds everyone seemed stunned...then the panic started. Some people next to me started screaming. Huge clouds of thick smoke billowed into the carriage. It was stinging our eyes and burning our throats. Some of the passengers were sobbing and others were crying out for help. There was real fear.'[20]

Such horrific experiences of terror—and their effect on wider populations, subsequently fearful that they too might be victim to future attacks—clearly form part of what occurs with episodes like 7/7. But is the deliberate creation and use of terror actually more central to what we usually consider to be terrorist violence than it is to other kinds of politically related, violent acts? I think this is an important question, and one which is all too rarely asked. Is the term 'terrorism', in its literal implications, helpful in designating what is centrally and distinctively going on? It is true that much terrorist violence is deliberately deployed with a view to the dramatic grabbing of attention, and that this is partly achieved through the psychological power of one act to generate fear among a directly or indirectly threatened population. But is this 'terror' mechanism necessarily more central to an ETA (Euskadi Ta Askatasuna, or Basque Homeland and Freedom) or an IRA (Irish Republican Army) bombing, for example, than it is to equally or more terrifying violence practised with political objectives by states in conventional warfare? Would such an ETA or IRA bombing be more centrally terrifying in intent, effect, and psychological dimension than, for instance, the 'Shock and Awe' assault on Iraq in 2003 by the United States and its allies? And while non-state terrorism has often been intended to make a civilian population live in a condition of fear, then the same would surely have to be acknowledged of many campaigns which have been conducted by states during more orthodox wars.

Moreover, just as in other types of violent struggle, there is far more than just terror at the heart of terrorist violence. A series of anti-Israeli suicide bombings by Palestinians will indeed terrify, and will do so with knowing and deliberate intention. But the dynamics of such acts involve an application of leverage through the use of terrorizing violence as part of a broader campaign of pressure. This broader campaign will involve the economic effects of violence as well as the impact of other activities such as propaganda, political mobilization, electoral campaigning, less violent forms of resistance, and so on. All of these elements are together designed to achieve political goals through the establishment of irresistible leverage, and this is also the way in which terrorizing violence operates as part of the wider repertoire of violent and other actions in conventional wartime. Is the ETA, Hamas, or IRA bomb more literally, centrally, and actually defined as relying on 'terror' than are, say, US bombings in some of America's own wars during the past seventy years?

Many terrorist campaigns arguably use violence in the Clausewitzean sense of warlike pressure: 'If our opponent is to be made to comply with our will, we must place him in a situation which is more oppressive to him than the sacrifice which we demand.'[21] The specific creation and exploitation of actual 'terror' is a part of this process, but not necessarily more so than in the orthodox warfare to which the Clausewitzean model might more usually be applied—in relation, perhaps, to the prolonged shelling of troops in trenches or the sustained bombing of military positions from the air. What I'm suggesting is this: that the literal sense of the word 'terrorism' misleadingly suggests a distinctively central role for 'terror' itself. An argument such as the following—'This is the essence of terrorism: the breaking of an enemy's will through the exploitation of fear'[22]—could equally well (or badly) be applied to the wartime campaigns of many state belligerents throughout history.

If the sheer range of competing definitions is the first problem to acknowledge, and the literal inappropriateness of the term itself is the second, then the third difficulty with defining 'terrorism' is what might be called the problem of the state. There are many who are explicit that terrorism should be defined as the action of non-state groups.[23] According to such a view, non-governmental, sub-state agents are central to the definition of terrorism, and, of course, such an approach tends to find much support among states themselves.

But the relationship between states and terrorism is very complex. Let's consider a specific example. In September 1991 my friend and colleague Adrian Guelke was shot by the Northern Irish loyalist paramilitary organization, the Ulster Freedom Fighters (UFF), at his home in Belfast. The attackers broke down his front door with sledgehammers at around 4.30 a.m., proceeded to his bedroom, and tried to kill him. Thankfully, he survived, two of the guns used by his attackers having jammed. But here was a seemingly clear case of a non-state organization committing a terrorist act. It now appears, however, that sections of the South African security forces had set my friend up as the victim of this attempted assassination, by persuading the UFF that he was involved in Irish republican paramilitarism (an absurd and entirely false allegation, but one which almost cost him his life). What seems to have happened, therefore, was that even in this apparently unambiguous case of non-state terrorism, a non-state group had in fact acted at the prompting of a wing of a state,[24] and such instances reflect the varied intricacy of the relationship between states and terrorism around the world.

For one thing, it's widely recognized that, historically, the largest-scale terrorizing violence with a political goal has been carried out by state, rather than non-state, actors.[25] The very origin of the term 'terrorist' related to the use of *state* violence or terror (in eighteenth-century France), and some of the most spectacular instances of politically oriented and modern terrorizing violence have likewise been practised by states (including those presided over by Hitler and by Stalin). States have practised terror directly; they've sponsored non-state terrorist groups; they have colluded with terrorist organizations whose interests have overlapped with their own;[26] and they have offered passive support for terrorism by ignoring action carried on within their own territory. Of course, states are non-unitary actors: it is sometimes the case that elements within the state apparatus may act in ways which are at odds with formal state policy. But the point is that, in all these various ways, states themselves can have a close link with the carrying out of terrorist violence. For some, indeed, it is of states that we should primarily think when we are discussing terrorism. The brilliantly maverick public intellectual Noam Chomsky has typically referred, for example, to the US as 'a leading terrorist state',[27] and has focused his attention closely on state or state-sanctioned violence, rather than on non-state terrorism.[28]

So I think that there are some problems with straightforwardly defining terrorism through reference to the identity of its perpetrator. Any serious analysis of terrorism *must* acknowledge that it has originated both with non-state and with state actors—a point made brutally evident in, for example, the Algerian War of Independence,

when both the French and their FLN (Front de Libération Nation-
ale) opponents used violence which clearly deserved the 'terrorist'
label.[29] And the variation of types of actor within each category
(the state and the non-state, respectively) has been considerable, in
terms of ideology, goal, lethality, and mode of operation.

In many cases, it might be observed that 'state' terror and 'non-
state' terrorism actually stimulate and sustain each other, and this
is an important theme to which we will return later in the book.
But it could also be argued that the dynamics of states and of non-
state groups respectively are so different from one another that it
makes sense to analyse them separately rather than synoptically (an
approach that will be followed in this book, which will focus on
non-state terrorism).[30] It remains important none the less to stress
that terrorism is not the monopoly either of states or of their non-
state opponents alone.[31]

If there are difficulties with definition by perpetrator, then there
are problems too with another sometimes favoured route: definition by identity of target. Understandably, many commentators have
focused attention on the identity of the victim (whether the latter
is randomly chosen, non-combatant, innocent, civilian, or some
combination of these): 'non-state or oppositional terrorism is most
usefully defined as follows: *Terrorism is the strategic use of violence and
threats of violence by an oppositional political group against civilians or non-
combatants, and is usually intended to influence several audiences*';[32] terrorism involves 'the use of violence or the threat of violence against
civilians to achieve a political purpose and have a psychological
effect';[33] terrorism 'is perpetrated on innocent victims'.[34]

But there are surely some difficulties here as well. The utterly
random selection of victims has often (mostly?) been absent from
what are clearly terrorist attacks. Even if we think of the 9/11
atrocity—in which the individual identities of the victims were
indeed effectively random—it's clear that we are not dealing with
a random choice of victim at all. Targets such as the World Trade
Center and the Pentagon carried with them a very precisely chosen message regarding the attackers' belligerence towards the economic, military, and symbolic power of their US enemy; in this

sense the identity of the victims was far from incidental, even on 11 September.

Difficulties exist also with the very categories themselves of non-combatant, innocent, or civilian victims. Imagine an attack on a military target, in which it is very likely that both soldiers and non-soldiers will be hurt or killed by the violence (since cleaners, canteen workers, family members, visitors, passers-by, and others will be in the vicinity of the attack, along with the soldiers). Are the injuries and deaths of the non-soldiers in this instance the result of terrorist violence, while the deaths of the soldiers are non-terrorist in kind? Is it really meaningful to distinguish in this way between different deaths originating from the same attack, or to argue that the attack has only been terroristic in its effect on the non-military personnel?

Again, there are clearly very different categories of civilian target. The civilian who happens to be walking past a café when a bomb explodes surely falls into a different category of victim from that of the civilian judge or journalist who is specifically targeted because of their hostility to the terrorists' cause. In the latter case, does the attack have a less obviously strategic quality to it merely because the victims of the violence are non-military? Again, a specific example might help to illustrate the point. The complexity of the civilian category is helpfully exemplified by the case of Sir Kenneth Bloomfield, an important civil servant for many years in Ulster, and the Head of the Northern Ireland Civil Service between 1984 and 1991. During this latter period, in September 1988, the IRA attempted to kill Bloomfield by bombing his County Down home in Ulster. In his own understandably mocking phrase, this was 'a brave military operation mounted against a wholly unprotected and unarmed civilian family'. To the IRA, Kenneth Bloomfield represented a senior figure within the governmental apparatus of a state which they considered illegitimate, oppressive, and in need of violent destruction. But he was clearly not a military target—'I was, after all, not a soldier, not a policeman, not a politician, but a civil servant'—and the Semtex bomb attack on his home involved a violent assault also on his entirely civilian family: 'The ruin of the principal target's house would probably kill or cripple his innocent wife and teenaged son.'[35] (A large part of the ceiling had indeed fallen on Bloomfield's son as he slept.) In the case of such an attack, there was clear strategic purpose on the part of the perpetrators as they threatened key people within the governmental regime of the enemy state, and the target was far from indiscriminate; yet the identity of the key and associated victims was clearly and shockingly civilian.

Nor is it satisfactory, I think, to argue that such attacks are terrorist purely because they involve deaths outside combat, since even many military personnel who are killed or wounded in terrorist attacks are targeted in non-combat situations (when off-duty, for example). So it would seem problematic to assume that terrorism necessarily and definitively involves the deliberate targeting of civilians, just as it would be perverse to deny that orthodox warfare has repeatedly involved just such civilian targeting (as in many cases during the Second World War). Indeed, civilians have been the most common victims of much recent warfare itself, and so the terrorist capacity to inflict awful suffering on civilian targets, and to do so knowingly, would again seem to overlap with more orthodox wartime practice.

If we can't easily define terrorism through the identity of the target, can we do so through reference to certain kinds of act? Can we define terrorism in terms of practical method, in terms of what it is that terrorists actually *do*? In the popular imagination, there are certainly numerous kinds of action that we might instinctively associate with terrorism (among them, hijackings, hostage taking, bombings, shootings, intimidation, kidnapping, and sabotage), so can we talk of certain deeds as being terrorist acts? The difficulty here is that most, if not all, of these features of the terrorist repertoire can also be found in other types of action, whether in warfare or indeed in criminal activity or conflict.

Moreover, groups commonly labelled terrorist typically do many different kinds of thing; and while some of these might indeed cry out for the 'terrorist' label, some of them (conventional political mobilization, propaganda, community work, criminal activity) do not. Even in the case of acts most sharply and commonly identified in the popular mind with terrorism—such as suicide bombings—there is some ambiguity. For one thing, only a small number of terrorist organizations carry out suicide bombings.[36] For another, suicide attacks extend beyond purely terrorist groups and situations to cases (such as Lebanon in the late twentieth century or Iraq in the early twenty-first) where the terms 'guerrilla' or 'insurgent' might be at least as appropriate as 'terrorist' in defining the violence which is occurring.

This leads us to a sixth definitional problem, which might be called the problem of related phenomena. Many terrorist campaigns are carried out by groups and movements which also engage in other kinds of violent activity. In particular, terrorism often over-laps with guerrilla violence ('an irregular war carried on by small bodies of men acting independently'[37]) or with campaigns which might be termed insurgent ('rising in active revolt'[38]). While some violence that has been practised, for example, in modern Lebanon, Iraq, Israel/Palestine, and Ireland might merit the description 'terrorist', it is also true that the practitioners of such action have at times been involved in activity to which the terms 'guerrilla' or 'insurgent' might justifiably be applied.[39] As noted, one profound problem in explaining and responding to terrorism is that it so often occurs as part of a wider violent and political repertoire of complex actions, as people engage not merely in guerrilla or insurgent campaigns but also, for example, in propaganda, political organization, elections, civil mobilization, and so forth. Distinc-tions here are vital—as one distinguished commentator has said, 'it is grossly misleading to treat terrorism as a synonym for insur-gency, guerrilla warfare, or political violence in general'[40]—but they are also very difficult. If an organization carries out some actions which are clearly terroristic, but others which probably do not deserve this label, then is it best to characterize the group as terrorist or not? To rule out of our definition those groups engag-ing in related activities would risk eliminating from view many of the perpetrators of terroristic violence across the world and throughout modern history (including, for example, ETA, Hamas,

Hezbollah, the IRA, the UDA, the UVF, the PLO, and other such organizations).

Guerrilla groups tend to be larger than terrorist organizations and to be more formally and openly militarized; they also tend more frequently to attack enemy military forces and to seize and hold territory. But even this does not always decide the issue. To many eyes in the USA, for example, Lebanese Hezbollah ('Party of God') looks to be a terrorist group. But is it an appropriate term even here? This Shia Muslim group (founded in 1982, becoming a coordinated organization in the mid-1980s, and aiming to expel Israel from Lebanon, to resist Israeli, US, and other hostility and oppression, and even to destroy Israel itself), has been characterized as terrorist by some scholars,[41] and it clearly has at times carried out terroristic acts (including the 1985 skyjacking of a TWA flight from Athens to Rome, and anti-Israeli/Jewish suicide bombings in 1992 and 1994 in Argentina and Thailand). Yet in some ways it seems misleading and constricting to define Hezbollah as merely terrorist. The group has large-scale support in Lebanon, numbering many thousands; it has embedded itself very deeply into Lebanese society, running hospitals and providing schools, as well as financial and social services; and Hezbollah has become very well organized in terms of conventional politics, proving itself responsive to the changing hopes and attitudes of its sizeable domestic political constituency.[42] Moreover, the Israeli presence in Lebanon has given Hezbollah something of the character of a national resistance movement: when Israel invaded Lebanon in June 1982, the Israeli invasion and presence decisively contributed to the strength of Hezbollah.

The ambiguity of the Hezbollah case is telling, reflecting as it does the complex relation between terrorist and other activity, and pointing us towards the fact that such groups, of course, can evolve. Hezbollah has developed from a more conspiratorial, terrorist-style group into one also engaged in more conventional politics and enjoying much support (increasingly doing well in parliamentary elections as the 1990s turned into the 2000s). By the early twenty-first century, Hezbollah had become a lasting and serious political player in Lebanon; as a consequence, it was one which could not easily be pigeon-holed according to any narrow label.

The evolution of groups from one form of activity to another suggests our seventh definitional problem: the problem of change over time. Some scholars argue that, in essence, terrorism has remained unchanged: 'Terrorism has not changed fundamentally in the hundred years that separate the beginnings of anarchist terrorism from contemporary terrorism.'[43] But it is also true that many books and articles, in different periods, have been written on the subject of supposedly 'new' terrorisms.[44] Just as terrorist violence has taken dramatically different forms at any one period across different regional settings, is there also therefore the problem that change over time has produced many different terrorisms, with the terrorism of each period requiring different categorization rather than being studied as part of a single phenomenon?

One answer here is to note that the existence over time of so many supposedly 'new' terrorisms might merely reflect the fact that terrorism is always changing and that—like nationalism, socialism, Christianity, and many other significant phenomena—it is protean in nature: that a phenomenon is ever-changing does not necessarily deny it coherent existence. Moreover, I think it's clear that at least some of the supposedly 'new' terrorisms have been identified after particularly jarring attacks (those of 9/11 providing a striking example), and therefore in an immediate context in which long-term reflection is understandably difficult to achieve. In the years immediately following 9/11, for example, reference has been made to 'the new type of global terrorism that has emerged with the attacks in the United States on 11 September 2001',[45] and it has been suggested that 'Al-Qaeda is the first multinational terrorist group of the twenty-first century and it confronts the world with a new kind of threat.... Al-Qaeda is a worldwide movement capable of mobilizing a new and hitherto unimagined global conflict.'[46]

In reflecting on such claims, however, it's important to note that numbers of internationally recorded terrorist incidents were markedly higher in the late 1980s than they were in the late 1990s, and that neither anti-American nor Islamic nor even spectacularly symbolic terrorist acts were, in themselves, new at all. The attacks of 9/11 were hideously world-dramatic, and they represented a novel form of terrorism in that they involved such a large-scale and serious assault within the United States itself. Yet, however understandable it is that these atrocities should prompt reflection about whether there had emerged another 'new' terrorism (this time jihadist, and embodied in the activities of al-Qaeda), there was actually much terrorist continuity between the pre- and post-9/11 terrorist worlds. The attacks of 11 September were by no means the worst excesses we have witnessed of violent massacre, and many of the supposedly novel and alarming aspects of the 'new' terrorism—religious motivation, or international scope, or the deployment of a new technology—are in themselves quite old.

Prior to 9/11, some observers identified the emergence during the 1990s of an earlier new terrorism, one that was religiously motivated, independent of state sponsorship, and less constrained in the scale of its violence; what had allegedly emerged here was 'a new and vastly more threatening terrorism, one that aims to produce casualties on a massive scale'.[47] Since the article containing this claim was published before 9/11, its argument cannot be dismissed as a panic reaction to that huge atrocity. Yet some of what it stresses seems less than genuinely novel. The 'emergence of religion as the predominant impetus for terrorist attacks', or 'the increasing technological and operational competence of terrorists',[48] could be claimed just as easily for earlier eras: religiously motivated terrorism had long been present, for example, in the Middle East, while the deployment of new technologies by increasingly competent terrorists had been experienced in Ireland for very many decades.

Indeed, one careful study of the 1990s new terrorism thesis (again written prior to 9/11) identified the essence of the argument as involving claims about a new terrorist network structure, new and more amateur personnel, and newly extreme and lethal attitudes towards mass violence; but it concluded that 'there is little that is new in the new terrorism, and what is new is not necessarily more dangerous or difficult to counter than the old'.[49] The supposed novelty of structure, personnel, and attitude tended to evaporate on closer inspection. But this study did acknowledge that 'the one thing new about the new terrorism is the increased likelihood of the use of CBRN [chemical, biological, radiological or nuclear] weapons'.[50]

Continuity accompanied change, therefore, even across the supposed fault-lines of the 1990s or of 9/11, and in itself the evolution of terrorism—in terms of advancing technology, for example—has been a long-evident feature of its history. But could it perhaps be argued that there does now exist a terrorism that is truly distinct and new, in the form of non-state *nuclear* capacity? This is a vital and alarming question. I think there's no doubt about the gravity of the problem posed by the threat of nuclear terrorism,[51] and some of the safeguards involved in superpower nuclear rivalry are absent from terrorist threats. If nuclear state A were to attack nuclear state B with nuclear weapons, then the assumption of devastating response offered at least some prospect of mutual deterrent; in the case of an attack by a non-state and elusive terrorist network, there exists no such retaliatory prospect, and this kind of deterrence is therefore removed.

Equally clear is the fact that, while most terrorist organizations are unlikely to attempt nuclear violence, there do exist terrorist groups which possess both a keenness to acquire nuclear capacity and also the ability to carry out a subsequent attack. Osama bin Laden, al-Qaeda, and associates have for some years been interested in acquiring the capacity to attack their enemies using nuclear weapons; they possess grander ambitions than even the 9/11 assault; and they have some members clearly able to organize thoroughly and to prepare very well for major incidents.[52] Nor is there any doubt concerning the horrific extent of the damage that would be caused were such a nuclear attack to be carried out: in terms of the lives, structures, and societies destroyed, the effect would unquestionably be appalling. A terrorist nuclear attack on a city in the United States could kill hundreds of thousands of people at once; it would generate dispersed and arguably unprecedented psychological trauma across a wider population; and it would represent easily the biggest and most catastrophic terrorist assault in history.

Terrorist attacks could involve the use of a pre-formed or a newly improvised nuclear bomb or an attack on a nuclear power plant or other facility, and the possibility of such an eventuality seems genuine. There have been recurrent attempted and actual thefts of the materials needed for making nuclear weapons (most notably, perhaps, during the transition process from the Soviet Union to Russia), and the possibility of further thefts seems real enough. Weapons and nuclear materials are currently accessible rather than theft- or acquisition-proof, and there exist many places in the world from which terrorists could acquire a nuclear weapon or the fissile material from which a nuclear weapon could be made.

How difficult would it be to smuggle a nuclear device into, for example, the United States? Only a tiny fraction of containers imported into the USA are physically inspected; and the smuggling of materials into the country is, it seems, comparatively easy. This is particularly relevant given that terrorist use of a small weapon or an elementary device is one likely option.

In the view of one of the most authoritative experts on this subject, Graham Allison, the position is profoundly dangerous, but not hopeless. 'In my own considered judgment, on the current path, a nuclear terrorist attack on America in the decade ahead is more likely than not. And yet I am not a pessimist. The central but largely unrecognized truth is that nuclear terrorism is *preventable*. . . . If we continue along our present course, nuclear terrorism is inevitable. But this is not a counsel of fatalism. Unlike the many intractable problems facing humankind, nuclear terrorism is preventable if we act now to make it so.'[53] Allison himself recommends that steps be taken to secure nuclear weapons and materials around the world, with the international community insisting that all such weapons and materials be secured and protected to a high standard in order to deny terrorist access to them; that there be no newly created national production facilities for enriching uranium or reprocessing plutonium; and that no new nuclear weapons states should be added to the existing list.

Preventable though it might be, the danger of nuclear terrorism is undoubtedly genuine, and it could be argued that the capacity for non-state groups to effect a catastrophic nuclear attack has grown considerably in recent years. To the extent that nuclear terrorism now represents the primary terrorist problem facing the USA, a new situation has, it seems, arisen. 'The possibility that a relatively small and weak non-state organization could inflict catastrophic damage is something genuinely new in international relations, and it poses an unprecedented security challenge.'[54]

But even anxiety about nuclear terrorism is not itself new, stretching back as it does at least to the 1970s.[55] And the gradual development of more lethal terrorist possibilities could be seen less as involving a different phenomenon than as an inherent aspect of an ever more grave potential threat. Nuclear terrorism would involve catastrophic destruction. But the dangers inherent in biological and chemical weapons—weapons that were potentially available to terrorists for far longer than nuclear capacity—themselves involve catastrophic potential; and even the awful prospect of, say, a chemical or nuclear terrorist attack on a state should be set in the context of what the historian Eric Hobsbawm has referred to as 'the extraordinary and terrible world of the past century',[56] a century which witnessed—among other atrocities—the extermination of millions by the Nazi and Soviet regimes and the dropping of nuclear bombs on Japan. Moreover, the threat of a new style of catastrophe does not necessarily mean that we have witnessed the emergence of an essentially different phenomenon. With nuclear potential, terrorism possesses a newly horrifying dimension. But, as with previous shifts in technological possibility, I don't think this produces a different phenomenon, so much as a still protean but starkly more dangerous one.

The final aspect of the problem of definition is in some ways the most obvious: namely, the fact that the term 'terrorism' carries with it such condemnatory and pejorative connotations. The word is almost always used to express something of one's revulsion at the acts one is describing or the people involved in them, and as such it delegitimizes the violence of those to whom the term is applied. 'The label "terrorist" works like that of the "outlaw" of old. It is value-laden';[57] 'the word "terrorism" cannot possibly be treated as if it were a neutral, technical term for a particular category of violence. The term carries a massive emotive punch. Indeed, it is probably one of the most powerfully condemnatory words in the English language.'[58]

In analytical terms I think this raises problems, since it effectively assumes a guilt or illegitimacy which analysis should ideally be establishing or disproving. The word 'terrorist' typically conveys images of a negative zeal, and it has powerfully done so for many years. Irish writer Liam O'Flaherty's 1920s short story 'The Terrorist' powerfully evokes something of this flavour, with its depiction of a monomaniacal and obsessive loner, scornful of society; an intense and terrifying exponent of a cruel violence which is to be directed at ordinary people; a frenzied and enraged solipsist, possessed of a disturbedly exalted imagination.[59]

Very occasionally, people do apply the term 'terrorist' to themselves and their own comrades. The talented early twentieth-century IRA man Peadar O'Donnell used the term 'terrorism' to refer both to state violence against his own colleagues in the 1920s and also to the phenomenon of Irish republican anti-state activity itself.[60] More recently, Osama bin Laden has spoken of good terrorism and bad terrorism, claiming that he and his comrades have practised the former[61] and that bad terrorism has been carried out by his opponents. (In 1997 bin Laden described the United States as 'the biggest terrorist in the world'.[62]) Broadly, however, terrorism is what others do: as one commentator has observed, 'Terrorist organizations almost without exception now regularly select names for themselves that consciously eschew the word "terrorism" in any of its forms.'[63]

Here, in a sense, is the problem with the starkly condemnatory aspect of this word. It's so easy for opponents to find cases of terrorizing and ghastly violence practised by their enemies, on both sides of so many conflicts, that one can end up merely with antiphonally chanted, mutually echoing abuse, and as a result with little clarity or analytical illumination. States condemn the terrorism of their non-state opponents, and vice versa, in an attempt to delegitimize. Thus Israel condemns Hamas as terroristic, but Israel's enemies merely respond by citing Israeli violence as involving a set of terrorist acts; and so the label can serve to obscure rather than to clarify, because each side merely deploys it in condemnatory rather than explanatory fashion. The UK state long referred to the IRA as terrorists, just as George Bush's US regime has similarly labelled its enemies in al-Qaeda; meanwhile, former IRA bomber, Marian Price, felt able to tell me in 2003 that:

> I'd never accept the term 'terrorist' for Irish republicans.... [But] I don't see any distinction between al-Qaeda and what George Bush's pilots did in Afghanistan. I would equate those two as terror, because that's what they were designed to do. Al-Qaeda aimed to terrorize the population of New York, and George Bush wanted to terrorize the civilian population of Afghanistan into surrender. And that's what America is intending with this war in Iraq, to terrorize the population into surrender. That's the real terrorism.[64]

The conviction that terrorism is what our opponents do against us, and that debate on the subject should involve this presumption of our enemies' illegitimacy, rather works against the profound necessity of full and serious explanation. To some, the term 'terrorism' itself might therefore be seen as an obstacle to genuinely dispassionate analysis, given that it is so profoundly loaded and condemnatory, and that it is frequently deployed in what are effectively propagandist terms. If the world is cast in such simply Manichaean terms, and if we automatically know who is bad, then little more analysis might seem to be required; and so the tendency towards understanding and explanation might duly become more limited. On this reading, the word 'terrorism' is merely a delegitimizing insult, and a means of ending rather than opening up the illuminating debate that we require.

In itself, I don't think there is anything wrong with casting the debate on terrorism in moral terms: there are grave moral issues to be faced, and anyone who has closely experienced or seriously reflected on what terrorist violence actually does to its victims will admit this. But there does still seem at least a potential difficulty with seriously analysing something within such an explicitly—on occasions, simplistically—condemnatory framework.

Given all these problems with the 'T' word, should we simply abandon it? If we accept the argument of one outstanding scholar of the subject to whom I've already referred, Conor Gearty, then it might seem very sensible to do just that: 'It may thus be most useful to call off the search for a coherent definition and to accept that advances will be possible only when we abandon the hope that there is a credible answer to the question—what is terrorism?'[65] Amid the plethora of competing definitions, and the difficulty of producing one which addresses the various problems identified above, it might seem that the term 'terrorism' has become an incoherent hindrance, rather than an asset, as we face the violence to which it refers.

Yet, despite his understandable warning, Gearty himself uses the word 'terrorism' in lucid and powerful ways, and he is among those authors who have shown that, despite all of its associated difficulties, the word can still possess considerable analytical value. Moreover, the fact is that this word is simply not going to disappear from the political vocabulary (it is far too useful to too many people for this to occur), and so we should probably retain our commitment to establishing precise, coherent definitions of the word, rather than merely jettisoning it. In doing this, we can be encouraged that many serious realms of analysis involve terms which defy agreed definition ('nationalism', 'revolution', 'democracy', 'socialism'), and that scholars in these fields rightly continue to pursue the most durable and coherent possible definitions as the best basis for inquiry.[66] Indeed, we might reframe the problem of definition by stating that we can never obtain a definition which is consensual and universally agreed, and that this paradoxically *reinforces* the need for any study to involve a clear statement of definition.

Because there are such difficulties with identifying those elements that are essential to all terrorism, there is an understandable temptation to assign different explanations to different terrorisms. As one leading commentator has put it, 'One possible reason for the failure of writers on terrorism to produce more incisive explanations for the occurrence of terrorism may simply be that terrorism, however we choose to distinguish it from other forms of violence, does not represent a single phenomenon and that different explanations of different terrorisms will take us further.'[67] Another way around this problem might be to avoid essentialist definition at all, and to opt instead for an approach that deploys the Wittgensteinian notion of 'family resemblances'. Rather than defining a word in essentialist terms—through identification of an essence, common to all of the things covered by the word—the philosopher Wittgenstein encouraged instead that one think, more flexibly, in terms of family resemblances or family likenesses:

> We are inclined to think that there must be something in common to all games, say, and that this common property is the justification for applying the general term 'game' to the various games; whereas games form a *family* the members of which have family likenesses. Some of them have the same nose, others the same eyebrows and others again the same way of walking; and these likenesses overlap.[68]

Along these lines, one could perhaps establish a set of features variously shared by different terrorist groups, thus avoiding the pitfalls of narrow essentialism while allowing us to recognize a member of the terrorist family when we see one.

Yet there seems something unnecessarily elusive about such an approach, and something necessary still about avoiding the different-definitions-for-different-terrorisms route. For all of its flaws, a more traditional style of definition of terrorism can still, I think, form the best basis for lucid, broad, and practical analysis.

Before finally setting out our definition, I think a few further points need first to be clarified. One is that, even if we dispute the idea of there being different terrorisms, it is clear that any serious definition of the concept of terrorism will recognize its *heterogeneity*. This is true in terms of the identity or character of the practitioner (non-state, anti-state, pro-state, state) and of the victim, and also of the associated ideological justification or political goal: terrorism can be of the left or the right, religiously inflected or utterly secular, revolutionary or favouring the consolidation of the *status quo*; it can be directed towards coercing an opponent into a change in policy, or concerned primarily with publicizing a cause or communicating a message.

Another important point, I think, is that terrorism might best be considered as a method deployed by people who collectively see themselves as engaged in a war. Despite sometimes being effectively dismissed from this category,[69] it is perhaps as a subspecies of war that terrorism is best understood, and the recognition of terrorism as a kind of warfare is indeed now reasonably common.[70] It's clear that there are major differences between orthodox warfare and terrorist violence, and I'm certainly not suggesting an automatic moral equivalence between the two. Terrorism does not involve formal combat between states; nor is it governed by the established rules of conventional warfare. But it should also be acknowledged that many episodes which are unambiguously recognized as wars have themselves involved frequent transgression of the established rules of warfare. And while it may be true that the 'essence of terrorism' involves 'the negation of combat',[71] so too formal war between states is now itself frequently characterized by an effective negation of meaningful combat for much of the time. (The late twentieth- and early twenty-first-century US assaults on Iraq contain many examples.) Much that is evident in terrorism—its unpredictability of incidence, its psychological-symbolic dimension, its ultimately power-political motivation—is also present in much formal warfare.

Some will object that to describe terrorism as a subspecies of warfare means granting undue legitimacy or credibility to terrorist actions. But I don't think that this is the case. Many wars in history might themselves be considered illegitimate and disgraceful, while still being acknowledged firmly as wars. And there are numerous good reasons for defining terrorism within the context of war. Not only terrorists, but also their opponents, have frequently seen themselves in these terms: in the contemporary setting, both George W. Bush[72] and Osama bin Laden[73] have presented the conflict between Islamists and the United States as a war, and so have others engaged in and opposing terrorist violence.[74] To define terrorism as a subspecies of warfare allows us to deal with the twin realities, both that terrorist violence can be part of a campaign which involves other, overlapping methods and aspects, and that state as well as non-state actors can practise it.

It's also important to recognize the centrality of *politics* and *power* to any proper definition. It is widely acknowledged that terrorism 'is fundamentally and inherently political',[75] and it is clear that it centrally turns on questions of power: 'terrorism is about power—acquiring it or keeping it'.[76] Power (in the form of violence) is deployed in order to try to achieve terrorist goals; and the redressing of what are thought to be improper power relations forms one element of the goal to be pursued, for terrorist violence is used with a view to altering the realities of political power in specific settings. As one of the most incisive of all terrorism experts, Martha Crenshaw, has observed, 'All terrorist organizations, whether the long-term political outcome they seek is revolution, national self-determination, preservation or restoration of the status quo, or reform, are engaged in a struggle for political power with a government they wish to influence or replace.'[77]

So, in response to the question 'What is terrorism?', we might offer the following answer. Terrorism involves heterogeneous violence used or threatened with a political aim; it can involve a variety of acts, of targets, and of actors;[78] it possesses an important psychological dimension,[79] producing terror or fear among a directly threatened group and also a wider implied audience in the hope of maximizing political communication and achievement; it embodies the exerting and implementing of power, and the attempted redressing of power relations; it represents a subspecies of warfare, and as such it can form part of a wider campaign of violent and non-violent attempts at political leverage.

No definition of terrorism will be flawless, but the above does help us to address the various definitional problems which have been identified in this chapter; it also establishes a strong foundation on which to build our interlinked consideration of the problems of explanation, history, and response during the remainder of the book.

The problem of competing definitions is not, of course, solved by adding yet another. But we might reframe this difficulty by stating that the ambiguity caused by the wide range of existing definitions, together with the impossibility of ever obtaining a universally agreed definition of such a contested term, paradoxically reinforces the need for any study of 'terrorism' to offer a clear statement of its understanding of the word. I hope that the definition offered above is sufficiently precise, supple, and fair-minded to allow for serious and fruitful debate.

The problem of literal terror is met by the fact that our definition acknowledges the significance, but not the unique centrality, of 'terror' itself to the process of terrorism. The difficulty surrounding the state is addressed through recognition both that terrorism can originate from state and non-state sources and also that the respective phenomena of state and non-state terrorism are sufficiently different in their dynamics to merit separate analysis (this current book focusing on the non-state variety). This also helps to address the question of pejorative connotations, since there is no inbuilt assumption within our definition that terrorism is what one's enemy alone does: according to the above definition, terrorism could be something practised equally by those who protect, support, condemn, or oppose us.

It's true that the term 'terrorism' will continue, even under this definition, to carry negative resonances, and to relate to violence perceived as transgressive of appropriate moral activity. But it does so evenly, and does not prejudice our judgement about any particular kind of actor in conflicts. Moreover, it seems reasonable in any case that the negative associations of the word should form part of our analysis, given the profound destructiveness of terrorist violence upon lives and society, even when carried out with a view to supposedly positive political change. Here, as so often, Joseph Conrad identified a major strain of the phenomenon when he focused on its capacity for naïvely attempting to destroy what currently exists, with a view to creating what ought to be: a terrorist, he suggested, might be considered 'a destructor of what is'.[80]

The problems of defining terrorism too narrowly in terms of target and act are, again, met by the above formulation. So too is the difficulty of related phenomena, as our account sees terrorism as something which can, and often does, form part of a struggle involving myriad overlapping kinds of violent and non-violent work: for example, ' "Terrorism" and "guerrilla war" *may* merge in variant forms, at times, in practice.'[81] The placing of terrorism within the category of war allows us to recognize its function as a mechanism—among others within a broad and varied campaign—for exerting leverage over an opponent towards political ends. That terrorists also engage in, for instance, political organization, sometime guerrilla activity, criminal acts, or other kinds of work, need not prevent our recognition of their terrorism. Indeed, it might only be within this framework that we can best understand what is actually going on: 'Terrorism is rarely employed by itself, without other accompanying strategies for gaining power.'[82] Finally, the problem of change over time is dealt with by our claim that terrorism is heterogeneous, that it can be seen as a protean phenomenon which has long evolved and which continues to mutate, but which still forms an identifiable and sufficiently unified phenomenon to be analysed as such.

Having established our definitional foundations, the next challenge is to address the related problem of explanation, and it's to this that I want to turn in the next chapter.

2

WHY DO PEOPLE RESORT TO TERROR?

In the summer of 1975 in the small Basque village of Itziar, in the northern part of Spain between Bilbao and San Sebastián, the local bus driver and alleged police informer Carlos was killed by two members of ETA. The shooting took place on his bus, in front of his sister and brother as well as other horrified and screaming passengers. After he was shot, Carlos's body lay over the steering wheel as the bus rolled backwards to a halt against a wall; his blood ran down the aisle of the bus and spilled out onto the road where it remained visible for several days. Numerous women who had just witnessed this brutal act immediately asked in pleading bewilderment, 'Baina ori nola leike?'—'But how can that be?'[1]

This response, of perplexed horror, is repeated again and again when we witness or hear of terrorist atrocity. *'But how can that be?'* Why would ordinary, local people—neighbours, family members, friends, villagers—practise such vicious, bloodstained, and appallingly final acts? *Why do people resort to terror?*

In public political debate, however, more energy, time, and attention tend to be devoted to condemning terrorist actions than to explaining them. In part I think this reflects an understandable, but still regrettable, instinct in the wake of hideous violence; and relevant here is the associated sense, shared by many people, that to explain terrorists' actions involves an inappropriately empathetic approach: that to explain is in some way to sympathize, legitimate, or justify.

But the task of scholars studying terrorism, and of all of us as we reflect on it, must surely involve a thorough explanation of why terrorists do as they do. To pursue such a goal need not conflict with a recognition of the awfulness of terrorist violence, or indeed of the illegitimacy and perniciousness of terrorist campaigns. In fact, if one really does want to contribute to the curtailment of terrorism, then the duty to explain the phenomenon seems unavoidable. Rather than seeing explanation as a justification for terrorist behaviour, I think one could more plausibly argue that understanding something is a necessary part of effectively fighting against it.[2] Accordingly, terrorism needs to be explained in precisely the same manner as we adopt in order to explain any other important, problematic, and complex phenomenon.

And I think there are two broad problems to be faced in regard to this explanation of terrorism. First, there's the problem that so many existing explanations contain significant flaws. Second, and much more challengingly, there's the problem of establishing what is, in fact, the best way of explaining or understanding terrorist activity. So in this chapter I'll examine the sharp insights and the significant weaknesses of various competing explanatory frameworks, before setting out an approach which seeks to draw on the former while avoiding the latter.

In the attempted understanding of terrorism, recourse has often been made to psychological explanations. To many people, the obvious explanation for seemingly inexplicable acts of violent cruelty lies in the psychological disturbance presumed to characterize those who carry out terrorist acts. But here it might be best to start by clarifying what is *not* the case. Research suggests that there is, in fact, nothing inherently psychologically damaged or psychopathological about those who practise terrorist violence,[3] and so explanation according to psychology is probably fruitless in the crude sense of trying to identify a terrorist psychological type. As one expert in the field has made very clear indeed, 'There remains little to support the argument that terrorists (from whatever background or context) can or should be thought of as psychopathic in the main'; 'Explanations of terrorism . . . in terms of personality traits are insufficient in trying to understand why people become involved in terrorism.'[4]

In fact, psychological studies have tended to stress the *normality* of practitioners of terrorism: 'terrorists, by and large, are not insane at all. The primary shared characteristic of terrorists is their psychological normalcy.'[5] This, as we will see, has profound implications for how we respond to terrorism. It suggests the inefficacy of a psychological-profiling approach (the pursuit of the chimera of the typical terrorist: a terrorist type which can be identified across conflicts); it points us towards the fact that apparently inexplicable groups carrying out violent acts are, in fact, well within the normal bounds of explanation; and it consequently reinforces the possibility that terrorist groups and those who legitimate them might—as rational, ordinary, normal people—be persuaded that other routes towards political progress make more sense than do bombings or hijackings. So I think that what initially appears depressing—the fact that appalling and extraordinary violence is carried out, in the main, by normal and ordinary people—might yet prove to be one of the more hopeful contexts for our response to terrorist atrocity.

That terrorism cannot adequately be explained through psychopathology now seems essentially unarguable. It could not, for example, be offered as a sufficient or serious explanation as to why there were high levels of terrorist violence in Belfast in 1972 but not in 1962, or in 1972 Belfast but not in 1972 Glasgow. Yet, while the attempt to produce a terrorist psychological template or profile might be fruitless, it remains true that the insights of psychologists—like those of historians, political scientists, economists, sociologists, anthropologists, lawyers, and others—can have much to offer in our explanation of terrorism.[6] For psychology clearly plays a part in any full explanation of why terrorists do as they do, and this is true in relation to the individual as well as at the level of group behaviour.

Any serious explanation of terrorism must deal with the individual, as well as accounting for broader group dynamics: not all young Basques joined ETA, even if they were sympathetic to that organization's broad political cause; not every Lebanese or Palestinian Muslim whose family has been harmed by Israeli violence has consequently joined a group devoted to violence against Israel; not every working-class Catholic in Derry joined the IRA in the early 1970s; and so on. Individual choices and instincts have been vital here in explaining why some, but not other, people have engaged in terrorism; psychological dynamics have played a significant part in this process; and so psychology can have much to offer in our explanation of this form of political violence.

The individual trajectories and outlooks of the central 9/11 conspirator Mohammed Atta and of the German Red Army Faction (RAF) leader Ulrike Meinhof were clearly important in explaining why they acted as they did. Where idiosyncratic individual interest overlaps with political cause, then psychological dynamics may perhaps be judged especially pertinent—'The way of even the most justifiable revolutions is prepared by personal impulses disguised into creeds'[7]—but at group level too, and in terms of ostensible political causes, psychological impulses play their decisive role. This is true in relation to the attractions and rewards of excitement, exhilaration, prestige, camaraderie, love, group dignity and belonging, significance, renown, glory, and power, all of which have played their part in collective terrorist activity. The psychological has been important too in actions which are partly explained by rage, anger, hatred, indignation, jealousy, and the desire for revenge—for hitting back and retaliation. It has been vital also in deeds which are partially explained by aggression, by an attitude of wanting to replace craven deference with defiance and to respond proudly to humiliation.[8] It's true that fanaticism, zealotry, exalted idealism, and enthusiasm are not unique to terrorists; but it is equally important to recognize that they do form part of any full explanation of terrorist activity throughout history.

And as our definition in the previous chapter made clear, there are intentionally psychological dimensions to terrorism: the communication of a political message to an audience beyond the directly targeted victims necessarily involves an enhancing of effect through a species of psychological warfare. Moreover, the symbolic nature of the targets chosen for attack can also amplify the terrorists' message through psychological impact. Such psychological combat, unavoidably waged in part with the aid of neutral or hostile media, can form a vital part of this war of usually weaker forces against their stronger opponents.

So while it is not true that terrorists are all of one psychological type, it can confidently be asserted that there are important psychological dimensions to the explanation of terrorism.[9] Indeed, some analysts have placed such impulses high on their list of explanatory factors: 'The most powerful theme in any conversation with terrorists past or present, leader or follower, religious or secular, left wing or right wing, male or female, young or old, is revenge.'[10] Such an impulse—conspicuous in Israel/Palestine, in the 9/11 atrocities, in the bloody cycles of Ulster violence from the 1960s onwards, and beyond—helps to explain why ordinary people sometimes step over the line from normal non-violence to a preparedness to engage in bloody and brutal acts. The latter often involve appalling violence against symbolic strangers; and the psychological impulse towards hitting back, towards revenge, also ties in with another psychological aspect of our story: that of group victimhood. *They* started it. *We* are merely retaliating. *We* are the victims, while *they* must be seen as the aggressors.

If the explanation from psychology therefore involves both flaws and important opportunities, then an explanation from civilizations again presents difficulties as well as potential insights. In a compelling article and a famous and powerful book, Samuel Huntington offered in the 1990s a civilizational reading of world conflict, to which some have turned for explanation after 9/11. Like fellow public intellectual Francis Fukuyama before him, Huntington's timing was wonderful. Fukuyama's end-of-history thesis pre-dated the collapse of communism, which seemed to provide its vindication; so, too, Huntington had published his case before the terrorist tragedy of 2001 made more widespread and urgent some kind of explanation for contemporary violence.[11]

In Huntington's view, post-Cold War global politics would be determined by clashes between major civilizations; rather than economics, ideology, or politics, it was culture and cultural identities which would now shape conflict. Amid multi-polar competition between seven or eight civilizations, he argued, 'The rivalry of the superpowers is replaced by the clash of civilizations';[12] 'The fault lines between civilizations are replacing the political and ideological boundaries of the Cold War as the flash points for crisis and bloodshed'; 'the fundamental source of conflict in this new world will not be primarily ideological or primarily economic. The great divisions among humankind and the dominating source of conflict will be cultural.... The clash of civilizations will dominate global politics.'[13] When Islamists attacked the United States so shockingly in 2001, this clash seemed to some to offer a powerful route towards understanding, not least because Huntington had predicted an intensified hostility between Islam and the West. The eminent philosopher Roger Scruton, for example, claimed in 2002 that 'Samuel Huntington's celebrated thesis that the Cold War has been succeeded by a "clash of civilizations" has more credibility today than it had in 1993, when it was first put forward. For many observers, reflecting on the calamity of September 11, the world has divided into two spheres—the sphere of freedom and democracy, and the sphere of despotism, "failed states", and religious zeal.'[14]

But is such an approach truly persuasive? Can terrorist violence, and terrorist campaigns, be globally explained in terms of a clash of civilizations? There seem to me some obvious problems with the approach. For one thing, the thesis tends towards the vague and the generalized, a feature evident from Huntington's statements that 'Civilization and culture both refer to the overall way of life of a people' and that culture and cultural identities 'at the broadest level are civilization identities',[15] or in his striking vagueness about Islamic civilization. The danger of overgeneralization is clear too in Roger Scruton's own elegantly formulated argument, as when he contrasts the West and the rest with the claim that 'Put very briefly, the difference between the West and the rest is that Western societies are governed by politics; the rest are ruled by power.'[16] The complex realities of global politics are almost certainly built on less monolithic foundations than such claims would seem to suggest.

This reflects part of a wider and unfortunate generalizing tendency within many existing approaches to the explanation of terrorism: the phenomenon is frequently discussed according to extremely broad-brush, template-based analyses which can blur as much as they clarify. In terms of the civilizational approach, for example, it is worth noting that the discreteness of competing civilizations can be exaggerated. In our current, post-9/11 crisis, it might be stressed that much of the thinking even of Islamist movements derives in part from ideas whose origins lay in the West: 'Islamist movements owe much more than they care to admit to ideas imported from the "West" they profess to despise.'[17] And much of the sharpest and most durable terrorist-related conflict has occurred within, rather than between, civilizations. This is certainly true, for instance, of Basque political violence in Spain,[18] paramilitary conflict in Northern Ireland, or radical-leftist terrorism in Germany. But it is also true, in a different way, in the case of much Islamist violence. For the genesis of some such activity lies partly in tensions between people whose civilizational contexts and influences are shared—as with Saudi-generated Islamism or with British-born jihadists of the kind involved in the 7/7 attacks.

Still, while any neat template for explaining terrorist violence according to a generalized clashing of civilizations should probably be resisted, it remains clear that the civilizational-cultural lens does have much value if it is used close up, and if we allow for attention to local or even individual nuance. It may not be true that what we face today is a broad clash of civilizations. Yet the genesis of some significant terrorist violence clearly does lie in the tension felt by at least some individuals between the centrifugal impulses of rival cultures within their own lives. In focusing on hybridity as the arena of cultural conflict, we might be able to sift out the more valuable elements of civilizational explanation.

We could, for example, reflect on the tensions between rival cultures felt by some disoriented individuals within culturally ambiguous territory. The narrative of contemporary disaffection on the part of individual Muslims in the West has been subtly observed and explored by novelists who have charted its intricate features, involving the competing demands upon the individual of rival cultures; sharpened lines of division and cultural and religious disaggregation after 9/11; personal narratives of insecurity, rage, and anger; and the resolution of ambiguous societal attachment and competing cultural demands through the clear and stark rejection of one identity and the decisive adoption of the other competing culture—'After a life of barely belonging, he is on the shaky verge of a radiant centrality.'[19]

And such patterns have traceable roots in the non-fictional realities of our own and, indeed, earlier eras. Mohammed Atta, leader of the 9/11 attackers, was a 33-year-old Egyptian town planner; the son of an Egyptian lawyer, he had studied architecture at Cairo University and had subsequently studied at university in Hamburg. Close scrutiny of his trajectory[20] suggests that Atta was caught in an ambiguous situation between a traditionalist Islamic past and a secular Westernism. Looked at coldly, Atta was unambiguously characterized by neither of these worlds, and a part of his route towards fatal jihadism involved a stark resolution of this ambiguous personal identity. Caught between sharply competing cultural-civilizational influences, he opted for a brutal resolution in the form of certainty and zealotry as a fervent Islamist.

I am not arguing that this fully explains Atta's career, but rather that it contributes to such an explanation, and that close reflection on individuals' experience of cultural ambiguity can at times be fruitful and necessary in our attempt to explain terrorism. There are other examples from earlier historical periods which support such a claim;[21] and more recent terrorist crises have again provided cases of individuals seeking to resolve the dilemma of centrifugal cultural-civilizational forces by means of fundamentalist zealotry.[22]

The latter phrase leads us to another broad framework for understanding terrorism, currently favoured by many observers: namely, the explanation from religion. Again, this is an approach which offers a mixture of very important insights and mistaken assumptions. Reasonably enough, scholars have noted the significance of the link between religious belief and terrorist activity. 'Religion seems to be connected with violence virtually everywhere,' as one distinguished sociologist of religious terrorism has recently put it, pointing towards the prevalence in numerous settings of religiously inflected political violence;[23] 'Religious violence appears to be on the increase everywhere,'[24] observes another insightful commentator. Understandably, perhaps, in the wake of 9/11 and the years of subsequent violence, many people have focused even closer attention upon the connection between terrorism and religion.

In separating the more useful from the less useful aspects of this explanation, it might be worth keeping several, partially overlapping, questions in mind. How effectively can terrorism be explained by reference to religion? To what extent are terrorists motivated by religion? In what ways does religion play a part in explaining terrorist violence?

There are those who suggest that the removal of religion would decisively take away a major cause of terrorist violence. One of the most famous of all critics of religion, Oxford professor Richard Dawkins, has made very clear his own sense of 'the evil consequences that can flow from religious belief and observance'; more specifically, in reference to the 7/7 London bombers of 2005, he has suggested that 'Only religious faith is a strong enough force to motivate such utter madness in otherwise sane and decent people.' 'Suicide bombers'—suggests Dawkins—'do what they do because they really believe what they were taught in their religious schools.' His broad point is that religion for many people trumps reason ('religious faith is an especially potent silencer of rational calculation'), and therefore leads to phenomena such as suicide bombings. If only religion were removed, then such evils would evaporate: 'Imagine...a world with no religion. Imagine no suicide bombers, no 9/11, no 7/7.'[25]

As a comprehensive answer in relation to terrorism, however, it is unlikely that an explanation from religion (especially from a religion perceived as divorced from rational calculation) will prove very effective. For one thing, many practitioners of terrorist violence have expressed no religious belief whatever, as with the case of many Marxists, for example: the 1970s terrorism associated with leftist groups in Germany and Italy would exemplify such a phenomenon. Moreover, even where religion does seem to form a significant part of people's views, its importance can vary greatly, and it offers only a partial explanation of behaviour. The IRA, for instance, has effectively been a Catholic organization in terms both of composition and of the communal grievances and support which have made it politically relevant.[26] But religious motivation, as such, was not the primary feature of its campaign, certainly in the late twentieth-century period; and it has been precisely the interaction of political (particularly nationalist) beliefs with religious background which has made the organization so important. The IRA drew almost exclusively on the Catholic community for its support. But its struggle was primarily for nationalist self-determination rather than for religious aspirations as such, and although its nationalism had historically been built on the communal grievances of the Catholic community in Ireland,[27] religion for the IRA has been one part of a larger and primarily political story.

It is certainly not true that religious zeal is necessary to terrorism, or even to that version of it—suicide terrorism, or martyrdom operations—most closely associated in the public mind with terrorist activity. Although commonly perceived as a tactic recently deployed by Islamists, it's important to stress that suicide terrorism is not new or uniquely Muslim—'Suicide terror...is neither unique to the modern period nor confined to any single region or religion'[28]—and also that it has been used by secular groups such as the PKK (the Kurdistan Workers' Party) and the Tamil Tigers (the Liberation Tigers of Tamil Elam, or LTTE), as well as by Christians, Muslims, Hindus, Sikhs, and Jews. (Though it is fair also to acknowledge that the radically religious do seem more likely than others to engage in suicide attacks, and that such attacks are more likely to target members of other religions than to target co-religionists.)

The crucial point, however, is that terrorism does not necessarily arise from religious zeal, any more than religious zeal necessarily generates terrorism. There abound many examples of religious zealotry which have conspicuously *not* generated such violent tactics, despite the fervency of belief and the grandness of global and cosmic aspirations which have been involved.[29]

Yet it is also clear that there have been, and remain, many terrorists who possess at least a partially religious motivation for their violent activities. Al-Qaeda has stressed the importance of its view both that the Muslim world is being attacked by non-Muslims and that this helps to justify its own violence and to cast it as defensive in character.[30] And if this reaction of Muslims to non-Muslim attack upon their lands is seen by al-Qaeda as defensive, then it has certainly also produced lethal, offensive assaults. Following 9/11, an Osama bin Laden statement broadcast on 7 October 2001 proclaimed:'Here is America struck by God Almighty in one of its vital organs, so that its greatest buildings are destroyed. Grace and gratitude to God.'[31] And it is clear that any explanation of the September 2001 attacks 'must acknowledge the fact that the hijackers were Muslims and that al-Qaeda, the group they were associated with, claimed to carry out the attacks in the name of Islam'.[32] Moreover, religious fundamentalism has frequently been central to violent conflict, as in the final two decades of the twentieth century,[33] and so there is some form of linkage to be recognized and carefully explained here.[34]

In the form of jihadism, the connection has indeed been spectacularly conspicuous. A figure such as Sayyid Qutb, the primary ideologue for modern jihadist groups and the ideological father of Islamism, therefore becomes significant as we frame our explanation of terrorism. The Sunni Qutb (1906–66)—an educated and highly cultivated member of the Egyptian intellectual elite—lived in the United States between 1948 and 1950, but came to consider US culture to be repellent and degenerate. Credited as the father of the modern militant jihad, Qutb is venerated by many radical Islamists across the world, and universities and Muslim clergy have been among those helping to disseminate his ideas. The jihadist wing within Islam was the one responsible for 9/11, and it has seen attacks on the secular world as a necessary basis for setting up the sought-after Muslim utopia.[35] Opposed to Western liberalism, and convinced that Islam is the one true faith which should consequently dominate the earth, jihadists see the USA and its (especially Jewish) allies as enemies and unbelievers. Such Muslim fundamentalists have sought to remove governments which are held to be corrupt and pro-Western, and to replace perceived Western-style laws in those countries with law more in keeping with Islamist belief.

Jihad itself involves struggle for the sake of God. This can be internal struggle to follow God and his commands and to lead a good Muslim life; but it can also involve external struggle (fighting) to spread the word of Islam, to bring Islam to all humankind, to support oppressed Muslim people, or even to overthrow what are taken to be false governments within the Muslim world. Jihad is central to Islamic thought regarding God's will for one's life and actions; but militant jihadism is far from the dominant reading of Islamic belief and practice, and it is certainly possible to see jihadist interpretations of holy texts as abusing their true meaning.[36]

A theological and political battle is currently proceeding within Islam and this intra-Muslim tension is an important part of the context for jihadist campaigns: 'Jihad is a concept with multiple meanings, used and abused throughout Islamic history'; 'there is no single doctrine of jihad that has always and everywhere existed or been universally accepted'.[37] So, to return to our earlier civilizational point, it might be argued that the primary battle involving jihadism is one within and for dominance within Islam, rather than between Islam and the West. Obviously, most Muslims have not heeded the jihadist call to arms against the West which has typified the approach of someone like Osama bin Laden. 'Most Muslims are not fundamentalists, and most fundamentalists are not terrorists.'[38] But while jihadist success should not be exaggerated, the at times spectacular violence associated with jihadism has made it a force of historical importance, and one which powerfully exemplifies the potentially lethal combination of religious zeal and terrorist tactics.

So it is necessary to stress that, here as in other cases, the collective and sustaining certainties involved in religious faith have indeed been vital to many terrorists; that, for some believers, particular interpretations of a religious text have reinforced or driven terrorist behaviour; that terrorist groups have frequently interpreted history in religious rather than purely material or secularistic terms, with God intervening directly in human affairs; and that in motivational, justificatory, organizational, and philosophical fashion, religious fervour and militancy have contributed to some terrorist action. In the popular imagery of modern terrorism, phenomena such as the cult of martyrdom have become prominent; it is unarguable that martyrology has been an important aspect of some terrorist campaigns, and that this has often had a profoundly religious dimension, whether Muslim, Christian, Sikh, or Jewish.[39]

Despite all this, however, it is also true that while a treatment of religion necessarily forms part of any full explanation of global terrorism, it is not a satisfactory explanatory framework in itself. It would be as mistaken to blame Islam for 9/11 as it would be to ignore the religious dimension of the jihadism which prompted the attacks of that day. And it should be noted that the leaders of the world's main religions oppose terrorism;[40] that Islam (like Christianity) possesses a certain ambiguity concerning violence; that the Islamic world is far from uniformly anti-Western;[41] and that sincere religious belief has frequently led people to oppose terrorism, as well as to endorse it.

For while religion can justify and intensify terrorist violence, the point is that this does not occur in isolation from other social and political forces and factors. It is only a very narrow understanding of religion which sees it as easily separated from other aspects of life: any religion of significance necessarily involves vital relations to politics, society, culture, identity, power, economics, and other potentially secular aspects of human life. ('Wherever there is theological talk, it is always implicitly or explicitly political talk also,' as an eminent Christian theologian told his students in 1939.[42]) Even in the case of Islamist violence, the explanatory power of religion is far from complete in itself. It's true that, while Islam and Islamism are different phenomena, they are not entirely separate from one another.[43] But it is also true that—even in the case of al-Qaeda or of Palestinian suicide bombers—it is the interweaving of political grievances and strategies with religious convictions which offers a more complete explanation for violence.[44] As we will see, it is arguably political, rather than religious, contexts and convictions which are the key variables involved in explaining terrorism; religion is on occasion important in so far as it relates to this broader and very complex political process.

Islamic fundamentalists themselves tend to favour the idea that the state is to be the vehicle of religious change, and they are therefore keen on controlling the state: in this sense they are profoundly political in aspiration. Even suicide bombings by religious people can be seen to possess an ulterior political impulse and rationale: 'Although religious arguments are used to legitimize the suicide bombings in the Palestinian case, it would be wrong to see the motivation as exclusively or even primarily religious. It is driven rather by a combination of *realpolitik* and despair.'[45] The interwovenness of the religious and political dimensions of terrorism can be seen again in bin Ladenism, which involves the simultaneous desires to expel the US from the Middle East and to construct an Islamic state which would control oil resources in that region.

To jihadists themselves, of course, there can be no separation of religion and politics,[46] and some see the separation of religion and state in the West as embodying the root of the latter's immorality. In this sense, Roger Scruton is justified in claiming that 'It is the very success of America in founding a common loyalty without a shared religious faith that so incenses the Islamist extremists.'[47] But while Scruton and Samuel Huntington rightly stress the important role of religion in our current crisis, one does not have to share jihadists' conception of the inseparability of religion and politics to see that significant religious belief and practice necessarily overlap with political motivation, aspiration, and argument: religion is not something that can easily be extracted from the other tangled features of societal life. Moreover, religion is not merely a surface, responsive symptom prompted by deeper, active realities: religious forces, convictions, and motivations themselves help to mould and determine political and other aspects of social life in deeply influential ways.

The most pressing current context for reflecting on this phenomenon is undoubtedly that of Islamist terrorism. It would be quite wrong to see Islam as a religion of fanatical violence or to consider religiously inflected violent struggle (and even suicide bombing) as uniquely linked to Islam. Islamic fundamentalism was associated with only approximately half of the suicide terrorist attacks occurring between 1980 and 2003, and Islamic faith is not inherently violent.[48] But it is Islamic political violence which most conspicuously and dangerously represents contemporary religious terrorism, and it is here that we can usefully see the value and limitations of a specifically religious framework for explanation. For even in cases involving Palestinian suicide bombers, where a religious dimension has been not only evident but prominent, one cannot understand the practice except at least partly in terms of expressly political grievance, motivation, and goals. Hezbollah and Hamas possess profoundly political goals, and their politics have a strong religious spine.[49] Lebanon's Hezbollah, for instance, has a profound religious base and dimension, but also repeatedly stresses what are essentially secular themes (economic, development-related, security-focused) in its politics and pronouncements.

Even the most famous of all twenty-first-century religious militants, Osama bin Laden, exemplifies the importance both of taking religion seriously in explanations of terror and also of locating religion within a broader complex of political factors. Bin Laden clearly possesses both a strong religious motivation and an associated political set of grievances and goals (relating, for example, to the military presence of US troops in Saudi Arabia, and to US policies regarding Israel and Iraq). He appears to have been decisively influenced towards his famously radical-Islamist path by the 1979 Soviet invasion of Afghanistan, a classic case of non-Muslim forces invading and occupying a Muslim country. The subsequent mujahidin holy war to free Afghanistan and Islam from Soviet occupation helped to bring about the establishment of a post-Soviet Islamic state in Afghanistan in 1992; and when the (US-supported) anti-Soviet jihad emerged within Afghanistan, bin Laden became zealously involved in it. He gathered significant funds, and himself went to Afghanistan to participate in the struggle: 'When the invasion of Afghanistan started, I was enraged, and went there at once ... I arrived within days.'[50]

Bin Laden famously helped to create al-Qaeda ('the base') in order to organize and channel funds and fighters towards the cause of the Afghan anti-Soviet resistance. He became something of a hero of the Afghan war, a conflict which was followed by Soviet troop withdrawal in 1989 (by which time the Soviets had lost 26,000 killed, and nearly twice that number wounded). When Iraq invaded Kuwait in 1990, bin Laden duly offered to bring the Arab Afghan mujahidin ('holy warriors'), whom he had helped to lead in Afghanistan, to defend Saudi Arabia. But the Saudis rebuffed him and opted instead to be protected by the United States, with the result that foreign and non-Muslim forces from the USA were stationed in Islam's holy land. Consequently, bin Laden was outraged, became deeply hostile to this Saudi alliance with America, and found Afghanistan under the 1990s Taliban regime a hospitable environment: a base for the base.

Safely set up in Taliban Afghanistan, bin Laden was keen for a jihad against the United States and its allies, and al-Qaeda provided the foundation for this initiative. In August 1996 he issued a 'Declaration of Jihad', aimed at forcing the US military out of the Arabian peninsula, overthrowing the Saudi regime, and liberating the holy sites of Islam at Mecca and Medina. He repeatedly threatened holy war, unless the US were to remove its soldiers from the Gulf.

Now all of this possesses clearly religious dimensions: the holy war, the Islamic struggle against non-Muslim forces trespassing on holy territory, and the defence of Muslims who have suffered at non-Muslim hands. Moreover, contrary to some assumptions, bin Laden has himself been preoccupied with the Israeli–Palestinian conflict, holding the American people responsible for Israeli oppression of Palestinians and interpreting the USA as a pro-Israeli crusader. Especially after the first Palestinian uprising in 1987, he took a strong interest in this situation, one which featured Muslims under attack from non-Muslim forces. But religious fervour here is inextricably interwoven with emphatically political goals. Driving the US and its troops out of the Gulf (something in which bin Laden has been encouraged by his experience of helping—however minimally, in practice—to drive the Soviet Union from Afghanistan), overthrowing the Saudi regime and replacing it with one that is more to his taste, responding to changing political allegiances and foreign policies when US troops resided in Saudi Arabia and when war and sanctions developed against Iraq—all of this is politically explicable, and indeed cannot be explained without recourse to directly political questions. In terms of goals as well as means, Osama bin Laden's crusade involves a religious brand of politics, and neither of the two interwoven elements here can be underplayed if one is properly to explain his and his comrades' terrorism.

So, to return to our earlier three questions (How effectively can terrorism be explained by reference to religion? To what extent are terrorists motivated by religion? In what ways does religion play a part in explaining terrorist violence?), we might suggest that a religious context is vital to explaining some prominent and important terrorist behaviour, but not all; that religious fervour cannot be ignored as a partial explanation for the activity of groups such as al-Qaeda, but that the processes involved necessitate that we also situate our explanation within the partially overlapping frameworks of political and other non-necessarily religious forces.

Before turning to explanation from politics itself, we should first consider another explanatory framework to which the case of bin Laden points: namely, that of strategy. Some leading experts have been hesitant to use the word 'strategy' in relation to too much terrorist violence,[51] and it is certainly true that terrorism cannot fully be explained purely within a strategic framework: as we have seen, elements such as religious belief, cultural or civilizational context, or psychological impulse can all play a role too. Moreover, as will be argued in the next chapter, terrorism has frequently been strategically ineffective and unproductive. But strategic thinking remains a vital part of any proper explanation of terrorist activity, even if the strategy should turn out to be an ill-judged one in practice.

This fits—indeed, it follows directly from—our definition of terrorism as constituting a species of war. For, as with other kinds of warfare, terrorist violence centrally does involve strategy: a plan of action with a view to achieving a goal, outcome, or objective. Highly intelligent efforts have been made to explain terrorism in terms of political strategy,[52] and this approach has been endorsed, at least in part, by many observers.[53] As we are often reminded, terrorism is a tactic: and this tactic is deployed within a broader strategic framework essential to any full explanation of the phenomenon. Terrorists have a goal, they are desperate to reach it, and their violence is partly instrumental—grounded in a belief in its efficacy and necessity as well as its justness.

What will this strategic aspect of terrorism involve in detailed practice? One feature of it is the asymmetrical quality of the warfare in which terrorists tend to be engaged. Typically, they are weaker than those forces which they oppose (though not necessarily weaker, of course, than the victims whom they actually attack); terrorists tend to represent small groups combating larger, more powerful opponents; and they lack sufficient strength to enforce their will through more conventional military or political means. So suicide terrorism, for instance, epitomizes the strategy of those facing well-protected and generally stronger enemies.

Terrorist strategic thinking can involve a variety of goals simultaneously pursued. Sometimes the aim is to communicate the group's political message: to make it unavoidably famous and urgent of redress, and effectively to place it higher on the political agenda. Several audiences can be considered relevant here. The opposing government is put under direct pressure by attacks; the broader public is targeted in the hope that it will exercise leverage over government, towards the delivery of terrorist objectives; the media provide a crucial amplifier for the terrorists' cause, case, and deeds; and the terrorists' own potential constituency is encouraged to support it as providing the sharpest means of cutting through to shared goals.

It is true that the publicizing of one's cause through terrorism need not be either easy or decisive. The longer that campaigns continue, the more mundane and familiar the violence can seem to a population or government which has become habituated to life under violent terrorist siege. And terrorist violence can, as in Northern Ireland, make the political issue both more urgent of redress and also more difficult to address amid a heightened polarization, mistrust, hatred, and division—all of which make the necessary compromises more rather than less difficult to obtain in the end.

But terrorists protest that they had no other choice except to pursue this violent route towards grabbing attention and forcing a resolution of problems and injustices: in this view, terrorism was necessary—indeed, essential—as the best or only effective way of pursuing the rightful solution to a problem. Examples of this abound, from the claim of one Tamil Tiger leader that 'The Tamil people have been expressing their grievances in parliament for more than three decades. Their voices went unheard like cries in the wilderness',[54] to repeatedly similar statements from Irish republican militants: 'At one time that was all we *could* do, that was the only avenue open to us, was to engage in armed struggle';[55] 'I think that it was inevitable that the nationalist people took up arms. There was no viable democratic alternative.'[56]

Such views are highly contestable. Certainly, in the Northern Irish case, most nationalists themselves felt that there was an alternative, constitutional, non-violent route towards nationalist progress, and they duly followed that route rather than the IRA's style of politics.[57] But the point to note here is not that terrorist violence was in fact the only available, effective means of achieving political goals, but rather that in explaining why terrorists have done as they have done, we must recognize that *they* felt this to be the case at the time. In this sense, recognizing the strategic conception characteristic of terrorists themselves is essential to explanation of their behaviour.

Such strategy can have short- and/or long-term dimensions. Some terrorist violence is aimed at the immediate production of a short-term outcome (the release of prisoners, for example). The most enduring violence, however, forms part of campaigns which take on a long-term and attritional quality. If the terrorist violence is sustained long enough, the strategic argument runs, then one's opponent will be forced in Clausewitzean fashion to accede to one's demands. This may, as we will see, involve a self-deluding confidence on occasion. But it is not any more inherently irrational than many strategic notions sustained by orthodox warring powers, and it can sometimes draw on prior experience to provide hope of victory. In November 2004 Osama bin Laden observed that 'We gained experience in guerrilla and attritional warfare in our struggle [in Afghanistan] against the great oppressive superpower, Russia, in which we and the mujahidin ground it down for ten years until it went bankrupt, and decided to withdraw in defeat.... We are continuing to make America bleed to the point of bankruptcy.'[58] So bin Laden's reading of Soviet defeat in Afghanistan—and of US responses to violence in Lebanon or Somalia—has helped to encourage the belief that his strategy can indeed work in grand manner against the USA in a long war. The experience of helping to drive out one superpower has encouraged him to believe in the possibility of defeating another. Bin Laden's al-Qaeda campaign is centrally driven by a strategic logic which is political rather than religious, although (as we have said) the two cannot easily be dissevered: 'Al-Qaeda is today less a product of Islamic fundamentalism than of a simple strategic goal: to compel the United States and its Western allies to withdraw combat forces from the Arabian Peninsula and other Muslim countries.'[59]

Strategic explanations of terrorism are important also in helping to account for the particular *kinds* of violence employed during frequently changing campaigns. This point can be illustrated by reference, for example, to suicide attacks. 'Terrorist groups appear to use suicide bombing under two conditions: when other terrorist or military tactics fail, and when they are in competition with other terrorist groups for popular or financial support';'all suicide bombing campaigns co-exist with regular insurgent tactics (non-suicidal bombings, shooting ambushes, stabbings, assassinations, etc.)'; and 'suicide terror is rarely, if ever, the strategy of first choice but tends to follow other strategies deemed less effective through the process of trial and error'.[60] In all this, it has been argued that 'suicide terrorism has a coherent strategic logic': it represents a particular brand of violence chosen with a view to advancing political goals. And such consideration is important when explaining violence in twenty-first-century Iraq.[61] Most Iraqi suicide attacks target military, governmental, or political targets; the unpopular US military presence and controlling power in Iraq are the central issues at stake and—to the attacks' practitioners—the basis for their legitimacy. 'While brutal both for the perpetrators and the victims, the suicide bombing tactic is not irrational';[62] 'Suicide bombers regard their deaths as strategic.'[63] Such arguments are reinforced by the assertion of al-Qaeda's Ayman al-Zawahiri that martyrdom operations, or suicide attacks, were 'the most successful way of inflicting damage against the opponent and least costly to the mujahidin in terms of casualty'.[64]

One other frequently significant element of terrorist strategic thinking is the deliberate provoking by terrorists of Draconian, counter-productive response by their more powerful (often state) enemy. Given the earlier-noted asymmetrical quality of much terrorist warfare, such intentional violence of provocation might often be judged to be the best way for terrorists to establish some momentum in their preferred direction. Lacking the strength militarily to defeat their opponent, they can none the less bring about heavy-handed state reaction (whether military, judicial, legislative, or other) in ways which can validate terrorists' own presentation of their opponent as repressive and illegitimate. This is a pattern frequently evident in Irish history,[65] but it is also one discernible elsewhere.

In all of this, terrorist strategic thinking may be misguided, and clearly terrorism is not explicable purely in terms of narrow, rational-strategic conception. Emotional, psychological, spiritual, and other considerations must also be borne in mind, and too schematic an adherence to strategically based explanations will probably fail. But the point is this: in explaining why terrorists do what they do, we must recognize their belief that particular kinds of violence make strategic sense, and that they tend often to act according to thinking which is no less strategic or rational than that of other actors in various conflicts.

One consequence of recognizing the importance of strategy within an explanation of terrorism is that it compels us to listen closely to what terrorists themselves say about why they do what they do. This is not to suggest that terrorists' ostensible and declared explanations provide, in themselves, a sufficient or satisfactory basis for explanation. They do not. And non-ostensible aspects of motivation—including personal ambition, rivalry, cultural disorientation, greed, the desire for criminal gain, and so on—must also feature as part of the story. But it's crucial to acknowledge the strategic dimension to terrorism, and to note that this part of our explanation will work best when set within the broader arena of what is surely the most important aspect of our understanding of terrorism: namely, political context.

Explanation from politics can, of course, risk downplaying the psychological, religious, social, and other aspects of our account. But just as it's central to a proper *definition* of terrorism to recognize its political dimension, so too *explanation* will fail unless we place political realities and contexts at the centre of our discussion, and deal with terrorism as strategically chosen violence within a decisively political framework.

Clearly, terrorism involves the pursuit of expressly political goals, ranging—among others—from irredentism, to regime change, to policy alteration, to redress of specific grievance, to maintenance of a fragile *status quo*, to revolutionary social change, to religious transformation, to decolonization and liberation from empire, and beyond. While we may doubt terrorists' claims that their violence offers an effective, justified, and solely available means of making political progress, we cannot dispute the fact that many terrorists themselves consider existing political realities to be intolerable, and that they think terrorist violence necessary in order to achieve essential change. In explaining the political, we need therefore to account for specific terrorism*s* within their respective local and varied contexts. The challenge here is to draw insights from other terrorisms sharing family resemblances with each other, while locating and grounding explanation within each ultimately unique context. Terrorism might be a transnational phenomenon, but its true explanation still requires sensitivity to the unique aspects of particular context, place, and politics.

Context-specific case studies are vital here. Indeed, one authority on terrorism has, probably rightly, suggested that 'in practice, the analysis of particular campaigns of terrorism or political violence has for the most part been more productive than the attempts at generalization about terrorism *per se*'.[66] But even when we attempt, as in this current book, to establish some wider points of definition, explanation, history, and response, attention to individual political setting remains essential.

One simply can't explain, for example, the German Baader–Meinhof group or the Ulster Defence Association (UDA) without attending to their very different social backgrounds (the former, for example, having been typified by a middle-class, university-educated profile, which was very rare in the latter), or their divergent ideological motivations. Again, the varying kinds of state (democratic, authoritarian, totalitarian) against which terrorism tends to be directed can have a decisive effect on the way in which one explains and evaluates such violence and the sequence of events which it is likely to prompt. Yet again, there are other important political distinctions to be made, as for example between groups with essentially localized goals and operations and those which in contrast possess more global ambitions.[67] If, as our definition established, matters of politics and power are absolutely central to terrorism, then close attention to political dynamics is clearly essential. Nor should this be taken to imply any moral equivalence between competing political forces: to politicize our explanation need not preclude critical evaluation of the political cases that terrorists variously make. The fact that terrorists are political does not mean that their arguments necessarily make compelling sense, or that their cause or violence is legitimate. And, indeed, terrorists' goals and analyses are frequently naïve, flawed, and deeply unrealistic.

Yet with politics, as with strategy, I think it's valuable not only to listen to what terrorists themselves say—however ill-informed or incoherent or brutal that might be—but also to take their various ideologies very seriously indeed in our analysis. The vital importance of ideological conviction—whether leftist and revolutionary, nationalist and secessionist, liberationist and anti-colonial, or drawn from many other significant forms of thinking—must be taken into account when explaining why so many people act in the extreme manner characteristic of terrorists.[68] Whether we are dealing with the Italian Red Brigades, Basque ETA, the IRA, or al-Qaeda, serious consideration of terrorist ideology is a necessary if insufficient basis for proper explanation. Frequently, such ideological motivation will involve the most profound disaffection from what is, coupled with a quasi-millenarian expectation of what will be delivered through violent struggle. And here the politics of legitimacy is repeatedly central. Capitalism to the Marxist, imperialism to the anti-imperialist, Judaeo-Christian Westernism to the Islamist, foreign occupation to the national irredentist—in each case what needs to be opposed is the existence of a perceivedly illegitimate political world. It is not that, where some people perceive existing regimes or structures to be illegitimate, one will necessarily find terrorism; or that such perceived illegitimacy in any way necessarily justifies terrorist atrocity. But it is the case that very many of the settings in which we have to explain terrorist violence are ones which involve profound problems of political illegitimacy; refusal to accept this will stand in the way of our successful response. Moreover, we have to explain why some terrorist campaigns (those of ETA, for example, or the IRA, or Hamas) develop weighty support and durable momentum, while others (such as those of the RAF or the Red Brigades) do not. And here it's worth stressing, I think, that the former have flourished amid a widespread communal sense of the illegitimacy of existing politics, while the latter have floundered for lack of such a broad perception among the supposedly supportive population.

Most significant of all, perhaps, is the political legitimacy problem associated with nationalist terrorism. From Spain to Ireland to Israel/Palestine to Chechnya and beyond, the explanation from nationalism is often decisive when assessing the most valuable framework for explaining terror.[69] 'Many terrorist groups and especially those that have lasted the longest, the ethno-nationalist groups, have been fighting for goals that many share, and that may even be just.'[70] Terrorist violence has often been generated by regional conflicts; and while such violence was deployed in the cause of nationalist, ethnic, or separatist causes prior to the Second World War, this phenomenon became much more widespread and powerful in the post-War era. Even in early twenty-first-century Iraq, nationalist elements of the Ba'ath Party have formed part of the terrorist and insurgent campaign against the USA, while contemporary suicide attacks (often portrayed as essentially acts of religious fanaticism) very often possess a nationalistic dimension, albeit one frequently involving a religiously inflected nationalism.

In much of the Islamic world fundamentalist religion and nationalism reinforce one another, and often enough what are seen as religious crusades are also, and on occasions even primarily, nationalistic causes. Islamism can involve a religious version of nationalism, and one that is rendered more powerful in its own cultural setting by this hybrid dynamism.[71]

It could be argued that nationalism represents the most powerful of all modern forces within human history, and very many accounts have been written as to why this might be so.[72] The tensions arising when boundaries of nation do not match those of state, when groups feel that their right to self-determination has been thwarted, when nationalities consider existing political arrangements to be illegitimate—the tensions within all of these overlapping settings have been the basis for enduring conflict, and terrorist violence has at times been part of this process. It has frequently involved hostility towards imperial or colonial powers, and the impulse against foreign occupation has been one of the most powerful dynamics behind terrorist campaigns: 'history shows that the presence of foreign combat forces on prized territory is the principal recruiting tool used by terrorist leaders to mobilize suicide terrorists to kill us'; 'suicide terrorism is virtually always a response to foreign occupation'.[73] It is not true that the politics of empire has always or only been practised by the Western powers which have held so much sway in the modern era, or that imperial threat involving a tussle between Islam and Christianity has involved only a one-way power relationship.[74] But in the period since the Second World War, much terrorist violence has been directed against the perceivedly illegitimate imperial power of Britain and the United States and their allies. What the latter call terrorism has very often been historically important because it has involved an anti-imperialist nationalism as well.

Within the world of political explanation we need also to consider the importance of ethnicity (which vitally, but only partially, overlaps with the politics of nationalism[75]), and also of broad social explanations, where factors involving age, generational tension, radical demographic change, relative group disadvantage, or other economic relations can helpfully contribute to our understanding.[76]

In conclusion, then, what *is* the best framework within which to explain terrorism?

Psychology, civilization, religion, and strategy do not, in isolation, provide the best lens through which to read terrorism or to explain it. But they do each offer insights worthy of incorporation into a broader, interlinked explanation. The latter must be primarily political: terrorism can only be explained within a political framework, and one which incorporates the wisdom achievable through attention to psychology, civilization-culture, religion, and strategy —as seen within a political setting.

This political framework possesses what I'll call *multi-causal*, *dis-aggregative*, and *dispassionate* implications, and I want very briefly to explain each of these in turn, before moving on.

Recognition of the multi-layered, interwoven nature of political explanation will necessitate that we reject monocular or monocausal explanation, and that we opt instead for a multi-causal approach: namely, one which links together the various elements of multiple causation which are involved. Terrorism is not produced either because of psychological impulse or civilizational-cultural tension or religious belief or strategic imperative but rather because of a political cause and context which can bring them all (and other elements) together. To attempt to explain Mohammed Atta *either* in religious *or* in psychological *or* in cultural-civilizational *or* in strategic terms, in this sense, rather misses the point. There is no single cause of terrorism (any more than there is a single cause behind other complex phenomena), and an interweaving of various elements within a political framework allows for an appropriate acknowledgement of what is 'a complex picture of multiple motivations'.[77]

In avoiding overly mechanistic, Procrustean explanation, we should therefore draw upon the various disciplinary arguments, methods, and insights available to us, rather than pursuing explanation within one specialist framework alone. Historians, political scientists, economists, sociologists, anthropologists, psychologists, lawyers, literary scholars, theologians, philosophers, and others can all view the phenomenon from revealing angles, and dialogue between such scholars is vital. (Despite its brevity, this current book has drawn upon work from each of these fields.)

So a multi-causal, political framework for explanation will place at the heart of the discussion questions of political power (often related to issues of nationalism, ethnicity, self-determination, and legitimacy), but it will not seek to separate the political from the other (for example, interwoven psychological or religious or cultural) features at work. In this sense, we should resist an approach which isolates terrorism from the rest of the political and the social world: 'terrorism studies', properly conceived, should involve a rooting of explanation within the wider, interconnected realities of political and social life. The formal-political will be part of the story (the pursuit of independent statehood, of a new government, and so on), but the strategic pursuit of such goals will not in itself account for terrorist behaviour: our account must be a thematically integrated one.

If thematically integrated, however, our explanation of terrorism must also involve regional and historical disaggregation. There is a diversity of terrorisms (albeit family-resemblant ones) to be explained, and so sensitivity to local, political, historical context is essential. Our definition of terrorism as heterogeneous and as centrally political points us in this direction: the only way to understand politics is to study it in historically and geographically specific context, and this is especially the case with such a varied phenomenon as terrorism. This reinforces the value of in-depth case studies, sensitive as they are to distinctive setting. But the ultimate challenge is to draw upon such specific elements while exploring the wider themes at work and the wider lessons which can, perhaps, be drawn regarding response.

The great differences between various terrorisms are as important here as the similarities which can also exist. Comparative study of a phenomenon such as terrorism can be fruitful both through demonstrating what extends beyond the local (whether there are certain patterns, for example, in terms of why terrorism emerges), and also through establishing what is unique in a particular context. Regarding goals, ideologies, methods, personnel, tactics, organization, and timing, terrorist groups can differ from one another in ways which underline the necessity of partly localized explanation. In this sense, the crude lumping together of terrorists as a uniform and single global enemy or problem is very unhelpful and misleading.

This need to particularize our explanation strengthens the importance of looking at what specific terrorist groups actually say about what they are doing and why. Only by incorporating such material into our explanation can we hope to understand clearly what we are, in each case, actually dealing with. But is there a danger that such an approach might suit, rather too neatly, the interests of some who have practised terrorist violence, by seeming to rationalize their actions and to disaggregate them in quite comforting ways? The IRA's Brighton bomber, Patrick Magee, for example, has told me that he was 'appalled by 9/11. For [an Irish] republican, the deliberate targeting of civilians is indefensible. Al-Qaeda not only targeted civilians but used airplanes full of civilian staff and passengers as a means of killing other civilians. I also oppose the suicide bombings of Israeli citizens.... targeting civilians must always lie outside the pale of legitimate responses to injustices.' Some might find these words surprising, coming as they do from one primarily famous for the fatal and crippling violence of the IRA's Brighton bomb. But Magee stresses that distinctions do need to be drawn.

> To see al-Qaeda and the IRA as being cut from the same cloth is a gross distortion that disservices anyone who wants to understand causes and effect. Al-Qaeda is an Islamic fundamentalist group that apparently believes that in pursuit of its objectives the deliberate targeting of civilians is justifiable. The IRA is secular, and fought the British state to achieve justice, and as a matter of stated policy and practice did not target civilians, although regrettably during the course of the conflict many civilians were killed by its actions.[78]

It is important to remember that the largest single category of IRA victims was that of civilians (642), and that the organization did kill many in awful and indiscriminate ways at times (such as their pub bombings in the 1970s). But Magee is surely right in his assertion that different groups need to be understood in differing settings; and the disaggregation of terrorisms into various contexts need not confer legitimacy upon the terrorist groups so studied. Indeed, understanding the varied roots of terrorist violence in its diverse contexts around the world is the only way in which we will be able to know what terrorism is, why it occurs, and how best to prevent it.

So the only way to understand, explain, or respond successfully to either the IRA or al-Qaeda is in fact to disaggregate: to know and to be clear about the specific, contextualized reasons for the violence occurring, rather than to lump together all such acts as 'terrorism' as though there were some generalized template of causation, impulse, and action which was universally applicable across the planet. In the Northern Irish case, an understanding of the IRA's particular goals, politics, strengths, weaknesses, and attitude around 1990—when the organization had recognized that its violence was not moving it forward successfully, and when it was prepared to consider alternative strategies—allowed for meaningful engagement by the state with this group, in ways that would not necessarily have been appropriate in all other cases.

It might even be argued that a refutation of the arguments of al-Qaeda or of the Provisional IRA would be all the more persuasive if it avoided any casual bundling together of these very different groups into the same convenient pigeon-hole and if, instead, due attention were paid to their specific and differing campaigns and attitudes in appropriate political and historical setting. In the end, therefore, I think Patrick Magee is quite right to say that distinctions need to be drawn; but such case-specific analysis is as relevant to those who oppose, as to those who justify, violent anti-state activity.

The best explanation and, indeed, refutation and response are also likely to emerge on the basis of accounts which aim to be reasonably calm and dispassionate. Again, our definition pointed in this direction, with its recognition that neither states nor non-state actors possess a monopoly over terrorizing violence. Calmly analytical explanation will allow for the fullest and most persuasive explanation, and might also in the end prove the most effective way of subverting the shrill, fierce logic of terrorist exponents.

3

WHAT CAN WE LEARN FROM
TERRORISM PAST?

On Thursday 7 July 2005 a series of bombs bloodily announced
the true arrival of the post-9/11 era in England. 'Terror Comes to
London' screamed the front page of the *Independent* newspaper.[1]
'Al-Qaeda brings terror to the heart of London' announced the
Daily Telegraph.[2] On 28 July 2005, exactly three weeks later, the IRA
announced that it had 'formally ordered an end to the armed campaign', to take effect that afternoon. The Provisional Irish Republican Army's long armed struggle against the British state, begun
in 1969, was finally coming towards an end. 'All volunteers have
been instructed', the IRA said, 'to assist the development of purely
political and democratic programmes through exclusively peaceful
means.'[3] IRA units had been ordered to dump their arms, and the
decommissioning of IRA weapons was promised to follow (which
it duly did, if not perhaps as openly or unambiguously as some
would have liked).

The events of these two July days underlined one of the iron-
ies of the new century, at least when viewed from Belfast. Just as
Northern Ireland seemed finally to be shedding its terrorist skin,
the rest of the world had discovered terrorism as its number-one
threat and as its dominant political preoccupation. To put it another
way: just as Ulster ceased to be Ulster, the rest of the world Ulster-
ized. Yet recent British debate on terrorism has often tended not
to draw on the past experience which is reflected in this irony.
Despite newspaper headlines in 2005, terror had come to the heart
of London many times before, and the problems faced by the
United Kingdom in the new century were ones with which it was

already very familiar from its experience of the IRA's violence in England. Unpredictable bombing campaigns in major population centres; the difficulty of a state trying to protect its people against such a threat; the existence of a disaffected ethno-religious minority within the state, within which a further minority was committed to using violence; a dangerous radicalization of certain younger people within this latter community, a process of radicalization partly worsened by the state's own efforts to address the terrorist problem; the difficulty in producing legislation appropriate to the new crisis; even the problem of shoot-to-kill allegations against the police force—all of these were themes familiar to anyone well versed in the IRA story, and all were now prominent once again within a different terrorist crisis.

If we accept the definition of terrorism which was set out in Chapter 1, and the interlinked approach to explanation which was just established in Chapter 2, then I think that there's an imperative to learn lessons from history. In particular, it becomes vital that we learn from calm and close readings of specific, contextualized, political-historical experiences. Terrorism has a very lengthy history: it is, as one author has put it, 'as old as civilization itself'.[4] Yet history has far too often been ignored in analyses of, and responses to, terrorism; and certainly the post-9/11 period has witnessed a frequently amnesiac debate on the subject, not merely in Britain. As one leading expert on the subject has crisply pointed out, 'since 2001 much writing on terror, particularly in the United States, has tended to neglect the long history of terrorism and counter-terrorism'.[5] In part, this is because many in the United States saw 9/11 as unique in a way which reinforced both a sense of American exceptionalism and also that wider tendency for states in crisis to assume that their own problems are so distinct that little can be learned from others' historical experiences.

But it might be suggested that, in Burkean manner, we should stress the crucial importance of *history* as a guide to our comprehension of current politics, and that we should do all we can to learn from particular past experience. This chapter will attempt to do this in two stages. First, it will examine what can be learned from

the particular history of terrorism in a modern Irish setting, focusing on the illuminating case of the Provisional IRA. Second, it will
assess the extent to which these Irish lessons can be said to resonate
with the wider history of terrorism. In each case, we will focus on
three major questions: *Why do significant terrorist campaigns begin?*
How are terrorist campaigns sustained? Why does terrorism end?

In addressing these questions, it could be argued that the Irish
case study might be particularly illuminating for a number of reasons. If we consider the post-1960s era in Northern Ireland, then we
have a historical episode of terrorism possessing a beginning, a middle, and something like an end. Unlike, for example, ongoing jihadism against the USA or continuing violence in Israel/Palestine, the
Irish story might therefore offer important clues as we try to answer
all three of our historical questions. (Some people might think that
the effective ending of terrorism in Northern Ireland makes this a
strange subject to focus on, but I think that the opposite is true: it's
precisely *because* major campaigns of terrorism have come to an end
in Ulster that the Irish case is so important and revealing.) Moreover, this Irish history embodies many of the themes that are crucial
to our global problem: bloodily rival nationalisms; sharp tension
between nation and state; the intersection of religion, nationalism,
and ethnicity, and of all three with terrorist violence; the partially
overlapping relation between terrorism and other kinds of political violence; and even, at times, the attempted fusion of socialistic
ideology with terrorist ambition.

Given all this, it might seem surprising that public responses
to the twenty-first-century terrorist crisis in Britain have been so
lacking in memory regarding what we can learn from Ireland, and
that they have tended to treat the problem as new, rather than as a
version of something with which we have long learned to live and
about which we have far more knowledge and wisdom available
to us than current policies might suggest. State policy on terrorism
and the vast bulk of the material published in recent years on the
subject have alike been characterized by a surprising and alarming
lack of historical understanding of the phenomenon, and political-
historical amnesia has hampered our contemporary response. But

the UK's experience of dealing with the Provisional IRA should, in truth, embody a very revealing history, especially if it is complemented by an awareness of the longer historical roots to political violence in Ireland, and of the actions of the other (loyalist paramilitary, and state) agents of violence in Ulster's post-1960s conflict. It may seem strange to some readers that we should discuss Ireland in these jihadist times, but I think that it will be very revealing to do so.

I

So what might we learn from this story of the Provisional IRA, regarding this chapter's three key questions?

Why do significant terrorist campaigns begin? The case of the Provisional IRA (a group established in December 1969, and whose violent campaign was finally brought to an end, as we have seen, in 2005) might serve as a test of our suggested approach: that of historical understanding based on clear, interlinked definition and method of explanation. The Provisionals can properly be explained only within a detailed understanding of the particularities of their geographical, political, and historical context—a point which would be agreed by all who have written seriously on the organization.[6] They were a group which carried out a wide variety of kinds of violence (including shootings, bombings, mortar attacks, kidnappings, robberies, intimidation) against a diverse range of targets. The latter included military personnel, police officers, prison warders, and civilians (whether chosen randomly or targeted because of their perceived role in the conflict). The IRA's actions centred on the waging of what they considered to be a just and necessary violent campaign; but even in their early days they were not merely violent: there was always a political dimension to their activity, as evidenced by the role of their political *alter ego*, Sinn Féin.

The Provos were born amid an immediate political crisis in Northern Ireland at the end of the 1960s, but their roots and explanation lie much deeper in the tangled conflicts of Irish and British history. The Act of Union of 1800 produced a United Kingdom of Great Britain and Ireland which was to enjoy only patchy enthusiasm from Irish Catholics, whose campaigns to amend or undo the Union involved both constitutional and violent movements during the nineteenth and early twentieth centuries. The revolutionary conflict of 1916–23 witnessed a formidable struggle between the forces of militant Irish nationalism (embodied by the political Sinn Féin and the politically violent IRA) and those of the British state in Ireland, the latter allied to their unionist supporters. Unionists—most concentrated in the north-east of the island—favoured continued membership of the UK, and were divided from nationalist Ireland for a combination of political, religious, economic, and cultural reasons. Each side in this Irish conflict preferred an outcome which would see the state representing their own national tradition (Irish or British), their own religious orientation (Catholic or Protestant), their own perceived economic interests (broadly, Protestant Ulster had thrived within the industrial, imperial UK framework more strikingly than had the more nationalist remainder of the island), and their own cultural leanings (more Gaelic-influenced for nationalists, more emphatically centred on Britain for unionists). There was, therefore, a long-rooted problem of contested legitimacy in Ireland, and the resolution of this in the 1920s was messy. An autonomous twenty-six-county state was established (initially the Irish Free State, eventually becoming known as the Republic of Ireland), partitioned from a six-county northern area which remained in the UK as Northern Ireland, and which comprised the counties of Antrim, Londonderry, Tyrone, Fermanagh, Armagh, and Down.

Long before the birth of the Provisional IRA, therefore, we can see in Ireland and in Irish–British tension a powerful example of the lethal potential of the politics of competing nationalisms. These rival nationalisms each involved the intricate interweaving of the politics of community, struggle, and power,[7] and they reflected the mismatch in Ireland between nation and state: the majority of Irish people were not, during the nineteenth or early twentieth centuries, comfortably accommodated within the UK state. But nor could a redrawing of boundaries according to self-determination neatly solve the problem. If the whole of Ireland were to be separated from Britain, then a strong and concentrated north-eastern minority of unionists would be in the wrong state and hostile to it; if partition were implemented, then there was no border which would allow for an exact match between preferred allegiance and place of residence. As the twentieth century was bloodily to demonstrate, the 1920s partitioning of Ireland into north and south left a sizeable minority of Irish nationalists in the Northern Irish part of the UK, many of them feeling that the state they inhabited was neither legitimate nor fair.

Thus the politics of nationalism and the problem of unresolved self-determination were long present in the Irish–British relationship, and they form a vital historical context within which to place the eruption of various terrorisms in Ireland. The political aims and justifications of terrorism—whether Irish republican (opposed to UK membership), or pro-UK Ulster loyalist—therefore had deep historical roots. In each case, there was for the practitioners of violence not only an urgent need for such aggressive action, but also a legitimation of it in terms of the nation: even though most co-nationals did not enthuse over your violence, it was still seen as essentially democratic because it was carried out in pursuit of what were perceived as historically legitimate national rights. The Provisional IRA in the 1970s presented themselves and their violence (they killed 1,045 people during that decade) in precisely these terms, pointing back for reasons of legitimacy to the authentic Irish republic which had been declared by the Easter rebels of 1916 and then embodied in the legitimate Irish republican parliaments created during 1918–21. According to this view, the IRA was

> the direct representative of the 1918 Dáil Éireann parliament . . . as such they are the legal and lawful government of the Irish Republic . . . The Irish Republican Army, as the legal representatives of the Irish people, are morally justified in carrying out a campaign of resistance against foreign occupation forces and domestic collaborators. . . . The moral position of the Irish Republican Army, its right to engage in warfare, is based on: (a) the right to resist foreign aggression; (b) the right to revolt

against tyranny and oppression; and (c) the direct lineal succession with the Provisional Government of 1916, the First Dáil of 1919, and the Second Dáil of 1921.[8]

In the view of the Provisional republican movement, it was the wrongful and colonial occupation by Britain of a part of Ireland (the six counties of Northern Ireland) which had ultimately caused the late twentieth-century violence there. Gerry Adams, long-time leader of the IRA's political party Sinn Féin, argued in February 1992 that that party was 'convinced that partition and Britain's continued presence are the core issues creating conflict and division'.[9] It was the British transgression of Irish national rights which caused ongoing conflict: 'The obstacle to peace in Ireland is the British presence and the partition of Ireland';[10] 'While British military occupation persists the Irish people are denied their right to national self-determination and sovereignty. Faced with this reality we remain committed to bringing the British government's undemocratic rule of the occupied part of our country to an end, once and for all.'[11] According to such views, IRA violence was not anti-democratic terrorism but rather democratically justifiable struggle in pursuit of national rights and freedoms. (A similar case could be made by those Ulster loyalists who used violence to an opposing end. *Their* right to self-determine their continued membership of the United Kingdom was felt to legitimate violence in defence of that goal.[12])

The arguments proffered in defence of violence by either republican or loyalist paramilitaries might fail to persuade most observers. But they none the less reflect the long-term roots of the political conflict from which (justly or unjustly) such brutal violence emerged. In the IRA's case, these arguments were made all the more powerful within the supportive community because the political was so closely interwoven with other aspects of nationalist experience. Irish nationalist grievance had long been grounded in and organized and expressed by an emphatically Catholic community; such grievances had—from the land wars of the nineteenth century to the anti-discrimination campaigns in twentieth-century Northern Ireland—possessed a pressing economic weight; and politics was reinforced too by a sense of cultural distinctiveness, as the politics of Gaelic culture reinforced a republican resistance movement ('Learn Irish, speak Irish, be Irish,' as the Provisionals' Belfast newspaper put it in 1971[13]).

So shootings and bombings in the Northern Ireland conflict could indeed be seen as terrorism, but they must be explained in terms of two mutually antagonistic political communities (unionist/loyalist and nationalist/republican), for each of which the interlinked matters of nationalism, religion, economy, and culture underlay profound belief and commitment.

On the Provisional IRA's side, it was considered that the denial of Irish national rights was compounded by a day-to-day unfairness within the British state in Ireland. Catholic communal disadvantage in the North had understandably prompted the 1960s civil rights movement for reform; civil rights agitation then precipitated inter-communal conflict, from which the turbulence of the Troubles subsequently ensued. So too, in the 1970s, the IRA claimed that the recent source of Ireland's violence lay 'in the social and economic deprivation suffered by the nationalist people' in Northern Ireland: peaceful attempts to deal with such problems had failed; the problem of such deprivation was maintained by British rule; and force was 'the only means of removing the evil of the British presence in Ireland'.[14] Daily disaffection, communal grievance and tension, and a sense that nation and state did not intersect as they properly should: all of these elements of the Ulster situation thus play their part in explaining the eruption of late twentieth-century violence there.[15]

The specific sequence of events which led to the 1969 birth of the Provisional IRA points us to other key aspects of explanation and understanding. One is the psychological and emotional force behind such violent politics. As civil rights demonstrators clashed with rival unionist/loyalist protesters and with police, and as inter-communal violence escalated during 1969, there emerged an understandable urge within some Catholic areas towards the provision of a new IRA defence force. But just as the existence, actions, and fear of the IRA had helped to prompt awful loyalist violence in the 1960s, so too violence from loyalists and then from the British Army after its 1969 deployment, in turn generated a nationalist desire to hit back. The Provisionals were rarely ever able to defend their community effectively; they did, however, succeed in hitting back: 'first, I think, was defence of the ghettos...and then to retaliate too. Defence and retaliation [were] the terms we used to use.'[16] With increasing friction between British soldiers and the Catholic working class, searches, arrests, and street and other clashes led to an increasing desire for revenge. Why join the IRA? One reason lay in the perceived harsh actions 'of the security forces within the nationalist areas...to strike back at what was going on in those districts'.[17] 'Why did I become involved in the IRA?', one ex-member later reflected: 'It was because of a process of British state repression as clearly distinct from any sort of attachment to republican ideology.'[18]

For some in the movement, ideological inheritance and tradition did, in fact, mean a considerable amount: 'I was born into a very staunch republican family.... So we always grew up with republicanism, and with a deep sense of pride in republicanism';[19] the republican movement maintained 'direct organizational continuity from [nineteenth-century] Fenian times, through the Irish Republican Brotherhood, past 1916 and the First Dáil to the present day'.[20] But this could overlap with an emotional rage and a desire to hit back. Future 1984 Brighton bomber Patrick Magee had an IRA grandfather, but he has also stressed that his own arrest and beating-up at the hands of British soldiers played its part in leading him to join the IRA: there was, he says, 'a sense of anger. Real anger. I felt I just couldn't walk away from this, and I did join up.'[21] In the words of yet another man reflecting on his own route into the IRA, 'Probably one of the deciding factors would have been constant harassment of British troops at that time on the streets. It generally created an atmosphere of violence and the desire to fight back and not to accept that type of state.'[22]

There was, of course, much more to IRA violence than such Fanonist rage. Reformist and constitutional methods of achieving change were deemed to have been futile and unproductive, and so force was considered essential in strategic-political terms. Interviewed in June 1971, leading Provisionals claimed, 'We hate to see the loss of anybody's life, but this becomes necessary in certain extreme circumstances. For a long time, various forms of protest against repression in Northern Ireland have been employed by the people but with little effect.'[23] Peaceful reform having failed, violence became necessary in order to destroy the unfair, illegitimate state: 'There was an accumulation of evidence to say to me that, really, the six-county area [Northern Ireland] is irreformable: we cannot change it.'[24]

Armed with a sense of the political necessity for change, and of the futility of peaceful methods, the strategic logic seemed self-evident. And this was a lesson (rightly or wrongly) drawn from Provisional republicans' reading of Irish history: 'Irish history is littered with the corpses of Irish politicians who genuinely believed that political processes set up by the English would achieve justice and freedom for the Irish nation.' But Northern Ireland could not be reformed: 'The six counties is a politically contrived and manipulated "state" designed specifically to allow the permanent domination of one section of the community over the other. Any reforms which it is forced to accept are only cosmetic in nature and in essence not worth the paper they are written on...The republican movement will not settle for anything less than British withdrawal.'[25]

To reach this goal, the Provos felt that force was essential: 'Only when Irish people turned to arms was the hope of real success raised.'[26] In the words of the Provisional movement's most significant player of all, Gerry Adams, in 1989: 'The history of Ireland and of British colonial involvement throughout the world tells us that the British government rarely listens to the force of argument. It understands only the argument of force. This is one of the reasons why armed struggle is a fact of life, and death, in the six counties.' Republican violence, therefore, was 'not merely a defensive reaction by an oppressed people. It sets the political agenda.'[27] Later in the same year, an IRA spokesperson was equally clear about the Provisionals' thinking:

The IRA strategy is very clear. At some point in the future, due to the pressure of the continuing and sustained armed struggle, the will of the British government to remain in this country will be broken. That is the objective of the armed struggle.... we can state confidently today that there will be no ceasefire and no truces until Britain declares its intent to withdraw and leave our people in peace.[28]

In the words of leading republican Danny Morrison, 'It isn't a question of driving the British Army into the sea. It's a question of breaking the political will of the British government to remain.'[29]

In all of these ways, the IRA fits very well our definition of terrorism, and its emergence as a significant group seems properly explicable within the explanatory framework that we established in the previous chapter. As such, its history points to some key lessons as to why serious terrorist campaigns emerge. The Provisionals for years used and threatened heterogeneous forms of violence with an explicitly political aim, and against various targets. There was a psychological effect to their activities and the impact of their violence, not least in their effort to exert pressure on a wider population than that which directly experienced particular violent acts. Ten years after they had killed their first British soldier, the Provisionals issued a statement appealing to the British people 'to put pressure on their government to withdraw from Ireland and no other young British soldiers need die in a war which the British government will lose in the end'.[30] As with bombs in British cities, therefore, so too violence against British soldiers was an attempt to coerce the wider public into pressurizing their own government towards giving the IRA what it wanted.

The political message was communicated to a wider audience through headline-grabbing armed struggle; and the pursuit of different power relations between nationalists and unionists in the sought-after united Ireland was pre-echoed in the redressing of power imbalances between Irish nationalists and the British state: the IRA was using force against a stronger power, as the perceivedly necessary way of weaker nationalists gaining their national rights.

And this could be seen within the context of warfare—despite the cruelty of so much IRA violence, directed as it often was

against defenceless and vulnerable victims. Why adopt the tactic of terrorism? Because such violence was judged necessary as
the mechanism for levering the British state into the concession
of nationalist demands. Bombings, shootings, and the like would
raise the costs (human, political, economic) of Britain's ongoing
presence in Northern Ireland, with a view to effecting the classic
Clausewitzean strategy of war alluded to earlier in this book: your
opponent had to be put in a position which was more oppressive to
them than it would be for them to give you what you wanted.

And so in explaining how the Provisional IRA grew from its
small, late-1960s beginnings to become a durable and formidable
organization, it's essential to establish a multi-causal framework. The
long-term conflict of rival nationalisms in Ireland is vital, as we have
seen, and so too is proper recognition of the ways in which such
nationalisms interwove not merely with religion and culture, but
also with economic and individual as well as communal, psychological-emotional processes. This has been made clear in regard to the
psychology of revenge and retaliation; but it's also relevant, I think, in
terms of those rewards which were available to paramilitary recruits
in terms of status, power, prestige, excitement, camaraderie, influence, and kudos among one's peers. Thus the civilizational-cultural,
the religious, and the psychological must all be considered. But the
overarching context for explanation must, ultimately, be that of politics. The IRA's goal (like the goals of their unionist, loyalist, and
British state opponents) was emphatically political, and the essence
of the Provisionals' early popularity was that they seemed to possess
an ideology which made sense of the emergent Ulster crisis. Traditional Irish republican argument had presented Northern Ireland as
necessarily unfair as well as illegitimate, sectarian as well as irreformable; traditional IRA argument had presented that organization as
necessary for the defence of the Catholic minority in the North. So
when the civil rights agitation for fair treatment was met, in part,
with hostile loyalist and state response, and when 1969 saw Catholic
areas attacked by loyalists and not satisfactorily protected by the state,
then traditional republican argument—of the kind now espoused by
the Provos—seemed to many to make good sense.

Ultimately, the Provisionals' argument should almost certainly be judged to have been flawed. As we'll see, the IRA's violence did not adequately defend Catholics in the North (indeed, it more frequently brought down more violence upon them); nor did the IRA manage to produce British withdrawal, or the socialistic change they so long proclaimed desirable, or the conditions within which sectarian division could finally be overcome.[31] But the fact that political arguments turn out to be misguided does not necessitate that we judge them to have been inherently unreasonable. The Provisional IRA became significant because, in a very specific time and circumstances, its politics appeared to make sense to people who were motivated by just that mixture of the rational and the visceral which drives other, less violent, political campaigns. One can doubt the validity of the IRA's bloodstained argument without assuming those who espoused it to have been in any way insane or beyond normal reason. In this sense it is vital to explain it—as it is to explain all terrorism—within a very particular local setting. The emergent Provisional IRA was very firmly rooted in lives lived in the experience of particular streets, and only the disaggregation of terrorism into such localities will allow us to explain it. If this was a story with many actors—British and Irish states which had failed to appeal to their respective nationalist and unionist minorities; civil rights activists who had prompted divisive turbulence; loyalist aggression born of insecurity and threat; police and governmental failures of response when the crisis arose; military heavy-handedness from the British Army, and serious violence from the IRA: all were involved—then it is also a tale which makes sense only in its intimately hostile Ulster locality.

Tellingly, therefore, terrorism here arose less as a simple, inevitable[32] function of communal grievance, than out of the tangled processes which response to that grievance had prompted, in the form of a civil rights campaign which had emphatically *not* been characterized by Provisional IRA violence. Similarly, while it is true that the IRA became a powerful force, with more recruits than it required, partly as a response to state aggression, it is also true that this state aggression was itself a response to prior insurrectionary provocation from, among others, the IRA. Moreover, a similar tale of complex origins and necessarily political, multi-causal explanation would need to be applied to earlier phases of IRA violence in which the organization had become significant, and also to those loyalist paramilitaries who opposed the Provisional IRA in the late twentieth and early twenty-first centuries.

If dispassionate analysis is necessary to explain the complexities which produced serious terrorism, then what of our second question: *How are terrorist campaigns sustained?* The Northern Ireland conflict, and the Provisional IRA's 1969–2005 campaign within it, between them provide a bloody and durable case study here: indeed, the fact that the IRA's armed struggle went on for so long is in itself a good reason for utilizing it as a test case of how and why terrorism can be sustained for long periods. One element in our answer must involve the self-fuelling capacity of terrorist campaigns once they, and counter-violence by their opponents, have commenced. It is not true, as Mark Kurlansky suggests, that, 'Once you start the business of killing, you just get "deeper and deeper", without limits.'[33] This is precisely what did not happen in the Northern Ireland Troubles, in fact, with the very highest levels of annual killing occurring early on, and with the later conflict being characterized by much lower rates of fatal violence. But there was frequently a tit-for-tat, mutually revanchist, dynamic to much IRA and other violence in the post-1960s Ulster Troubles. As suggested, this played a part in the emergence of the Provisional IRA as a serious force in the first place. In June 1970 Protestant Orange Order parading on the edge of Belfast's Catholic Ardoyne provoked clashes between the two communities, in which the IRA killed three Protestants. Later on the same day, a Catholic area within largely Protestant east Belfast was attacked, and a lengthy gun battle resulted. The state responded by embarking on what became known as the Falls curfew: an extensive search of Belfast's nationalist Lower Falls area by British troops in early July. Rioting ensued, a curfew was introduced, houses were damaged during searches, and a number of people were killed. Many weapons were indeed found by the Army; but it is also true that this episode seriously worsened relations between the Catholic working class and the British forces. In Gerry Adams's words, 'The Falls Road curfew in July 1970 made popular opposition to the British Army absolute in Belfast... After that recruitment to the IRA was massive.'[34]

Matters deteriorated speedily: indeed, one of the lessons of these bloody years in Northern Ireland is just how quickly peace can descend into something like war. In 1968 nobody died as a result of political violence in the North; in 1972, the Troubles cost 497 lives. The escalation in these years grew from multiple causes. By October 1970 the Provisional IRA was in a position to embark on a full offensive, and during that month it began a serious bombing campaign. At the start of 1971 the Provos' ruling Army Council sanctioned operations directly against the British Army, and the IRA duly began systematically to shoot at troops in Belfast (the first fatal shooting taking place in early February). From then until August 1971 the contest between the IRA and the Army grew fiercely, and in the latter month the Northern Ireland unionist government pressurized London towards introducing internment without trial as a means of attempting to contain the violent crisis. Thus it was that on 9 August 1971 hundreds of people were lifted—most of them members of neither the Provisional nor the rival Official IRA. Initial swoops were aimed at republicans alone, a one-sidedness which unsurprisingly angered many within the nationalist community.

Interning non-involved civilians on the basis of weak intelligence was a mistake compounded by the harsh treatment which some internees subsequently endured. Rather than undermining the IRA, this internment initiative helped to strengthen it and to increase its capacity for brutal violence. During the pre-internment period of 1971 (up to 9 August) the Provisional IRA killed ten British soldiers; during the remaining months of the year it killed thirty. When British soldiers fatally shot fourteen Catholic civilians at an anti-internment march on 30 January 1972 in Derry ('Bloody Sunday'), the hostility between the IRA and the authorities became more intense still, and the IRA had more potential recruits than it could easily cope with. It was not that state violence alone had produced this situation (republican and loyalist brutality and intention had, along with other factors, played their part too); nor was it that any one incident on its own produced the crisis. But the cumulative experience of bloodstained friction seemed to each side to justify and necessitate violence in return, and one result was that the IRA grew to become a serious force. In particular, it might be noted that state violence against civilians played a dramatic part in stimulating the growth of precisely that organization against which the state action had been directed.

The sustenance of terrorism through the self-fuelling dynamics of violence can again and again be seen during the years of the Northern Ireland Troubles. Some of the most hideous late twentieth-century Ulster violence occurred in the mid-1970s in south Armagh, with loyalists and republicans each seeking vengeance for the killings carried out by the other side beforehand, in a cycle which claimed many lives. In August 1975, for example, and again in January 1976, there were cruel sequences of killing, tit-for-tat episodes of revanchist, responsive murder by republicans and loyalists in turn. Similarly self-sustaining patterns of violence can be seen in the grim catalogue of killing from the early 1990s. In September 1993 the republican paper *An Phoblacht/Republican News* referred to the loyalist murder of Catholics by 'sectarian death squads', while earlier in the year the IRA had killed alleged Ulster Volunteer Force (UVF) organizer Matthew John Boyd, from County Tyrone, claiming that 'Boyd had a long involvement in the UVF dating back to the 1970s...his increasingly crucial role in UVF sectarian murders became clear and IRA intelligence had him under surveillance along with several other UVF personnel...we will execute those involved in sectarian killings.'[35]

Just as the modern UVF, therefore, had emerged in response to loyalist anxiety about the Irish republican threat,[36] so too the IRA responded to loyalist violence with its own violent action. On Saturday 23 October 1993 an IRA bomb exploded on the Protestant Shankill Road in Belfast, its ostensible target being an Ulster Defence Association (UDA) meeting mistakenly thought by the IRA to have been taking place above the shop where the bomb exploded. One of the bombers was killed, along with nine Protestants (none of whom were paramilitaries). This attack had been preceded and prompted by a recent series of UDA/UFF killings of Catholics. Its effect, however, was to generate in turn even higher levels of loyalist violence: in the month before the IRA's Shankill bombing, loyalists killed three people; in the vengeful month which followed the bomb, loyalists retaliated by killing thirteen.

So for all of those carrying out violence in the North during the Troubles—republicans, loyalists, and state forces—one sustaining feature was the banal one of other people's violence, directed towards people like yourself. This is a lesson taught also by earlier phases of violent Irish history,[37] and it clearly relates to our earlier stress upon the psychological and emotional aspects of terrorist violence. When at Warrenpoint in 1979 the IRA killed eighteen members of the Parachute Regiment (the Regiment responsible for the Bloody Sunday killings in Derry seven years earlier), and on the same day killed Lord Mountbatten, republican prisoners in the H-blocks of the Maze Prison responded with 'euphoria' and 'elation'.[38] When republican prisoners were engaged in their hunger strike during 1981 in the same Maze jail, IRA inmates looked for widespread killing in response: 'There was disappointment that the IRA response to the hunger-strike deaths wasn't what it should have been... We felt that the IRA could have been slaughtering these people in twenties and thirties; we were expecting Warrenpoints and hoping for Warrenpoints, 'cos the people were dying in the jails.'[39]

The violence of one's opponents, in this Northern Irish case, seemed both to validate and to necessitate an aggressive response, which in turn stimulated counter-response, and so on. To this inter-communal hostility could be added the sustaining role played by *intra*-communal violence. Within the Irish republican movement there repeatedly developed feuds and splits, as the IRA split into warring Provisional and Official factions, and as the latter then spawned a hostile offshoot in the form of the Irish National Liberation Army (INLA).[40] In these intra-movement battles tit-for-tat vengeance played a part, as did rival conceptions of the best strategic or ideological path, and competition between alternative leaders and leaderships. Similar intra-communal struggles were apparent also on the loyalist side of Northern Ireland's divided community, and again played their self-sustaining part in maintaining terrorist violence.

A second crucial element in sustaining terrorist political violence, however, lies in the degree of sustained political commitment and belief exhibited by those involved. If—as I have argued—we should recognize the ineluctably political nature of terrorism, and if we can explain terrorism properly only by reference to this reality, then it's important to acknowledge that long-term terrorist campaigns endure in part because of the sincere political commitment of those who are involved, and because of the seriousness of the political problems around which their campaigns have emerged.

One aspect of this involves terrorists' tough-minded preparedness to wage war for many years, as was evident from the Provisional IRA's own long struggle. Part of it also relies, crucially, on the group's belief that violence is indeed having an effect or at least promises the likelihood of doing so. In the early- and mid-1970s many Provisionals did believe that victory was potentially imminent: 1974 was to be 'the year of liberty',[41] for example, while in early 1976 the Provos declared that 'During the past year there have been ample indications that Britain is accelerating her plan for total withdrawal from the six counties.'[42]

Such hopes proved illusory, and the IRA opted for a 'long war' strategy in the latter half of the 1970s. Some Provisional leaders had even before this recognized that the struggle was likely to be a lengthy one; Gerry Adams certainly appears to have been prepared for twenty years of warlike conflict as early as 1973.[43] But the important point here is that such anticipation of long-term conflict was again based on the expectation of ultimate victory. This might have been naïve, but it was seriously and sincerely held, and it is crucial to explaining why the IRA did as it did for so long. 'Make no mistake about it... Britain's days in Ireland are numbered';[44] 'That the British face military defeat is inevitable and obvious.'[45]

So the war was not only just, in terms of Irish rights to national self-determination and to liberation from colonial enslavement:

it was also destined for success, as suggested by the tide of late twentieth-century decline experienced by the British Empire. Such beliefs were the foundation for the enduring IRA campaign. Sustenance could also be provided by other kinds of belief (cultural-nationalist enthusiasm for some, socialist millenarianism for others, ideological strength taken from republican history for yet more); it could also come through support from external actors (whether diasporic sympathizers in the USA or regimes such as Colonel Gaddafi's Libya which shared a hostility towards the Provisionals' UK enemy); and struggle could partly be sustained by some of those psychological-emotional rewards to which our earlier argument has pointed: the attractions of power, excitement, adventure, enhanced influence, prestige, identity, solidarity, comradeship, and purposeful soldiership.

A third sustaining element in the Provisionals' long campaign lay in the more mundane but significant momentum provided by organizational dynamics themselves. Just as state hostility could prompt and intensify republican resistance and determination, so too training, organizational responsibilities, meetings, campaigning, fund-raising, commemorations, and the like themselves helped to make the war last.

In this sense, the mechanics of struggle themselves were partly self-sustaining, even self-validating. The 1976–81 prison conflict over whether republican inmates should be seen as criminal (the UK authorities' preference) or political (as demanded by the prisoners themselves) provided one fierce setting for this, with widespread mobilization within and beyond the jails, considerable publicity and propaganda and international cause promotion, and an escalation of organizational resistance focused on the prison experience. The organization of prisoner-centred struggle, like the practicalities of fund-raising or arms procurement, or the associated political work which long accompanied IRA violence—all of these mechanical processes possessed a certain self-sustaining capacity.

But they would only be feasible as part of a long-term war if there were people who were willing and able to lead such a struggle. Leaders had, at low points in Irish republican history, on occasion been effectively the only ones to keep the movement alive. There was something of this, for example, in the period from the 1940s through to the 1960s for the IRA. Leaders could provide the day-to-day foundation for the group's activities, but they could also inspire, influence, mentor, intimidate, and direct. Some leading figures derived their importance within the Provisional movement from their enduring and changing role over many years (Martin McGuinness and Gerry Adams provide the most obvious examples); others were durably influential and inspiring in death (1981 hunger-striker Bobby Sands being the pre-eminent figure here).

A campaign such as the IRA's, therefore, endured because of the political commitment and belief of those involved, the self-fuelling effect of violence itself, the momentum gained from organizational dynamics, and the directional role and influence of leaders. And it's important here to stress that the sustenance of major, durable terrorist campaigns such as that of the Provisional IRA is no easy matter to achieve. During the IRA's violent campaign, most nationalists in the North of Ireland (and most Irish nationalists elsewhere) did not support the Provos' violence. Prior to the IRA's cessation of violence, it was their constitutional nationalist rivals the Social Democratic and Labour Party (SDLP) who repeatedly and emphatically gained the majority of support from northern nationalists.[46]

Without doubt, the clumsy response of the British state helped to sustain IRA zealotry. (Would it have been anything like so enduring and significant without the 1970 Falls curfew, 1971 internment, Bloody Sunday in 1972, and the avoidable 1981 hunger strike?) But it is also vital to acknowledge that, while most nationalists eschewed the Provisionals' murderous politics while it was being practised, the central issues over which the IRA was fighting—the interwoven questions of northern nationalists' rights and Irish national self-determination—were ones which did, in fact, resonate with large numbers of Irish nationalists in Ulster and beyond. One cannot explain the durability of the Provos' brutal campaign without acknowledging that there was, behind it, a serious and recognizably important contest over political legitimacy.

Multiple causation is clearly at work, therefore, in the generation and sustenance of terrorism, and the same is true when we turn to our third major question: *Why does terrorism end?* 'Even conflicts that appear to be intractable can eventually be brought to an end.'[47] So claimed long-time Sinn Féin leader Gerry Adams in 1995, and his own role in the long trajectory of Provisional republicanism— through violent eruption, long conflict, and eventual cessation— has been crucial. Some observers of terrorist campaigns tend to stress that they can end only when the terrorists are unambiguously defeated; a contrasting school of thought suggests that terrorism can be brought to an end only by initiating a peace process to which terrorists and their followers can then respond, thereby ending the violence. The lessons from Northern Ireland and the end of the IRA's campaign fit neither of these views particularly neatly, and this is another reason for spending some time addressing the Irish case. For what happened there was rather that Irish republican leaders in the late 1980s came to the view that their violence was not producing the victory which they had initially and long anticipated; and that they duly considered that armed struggle might— eventually—be better replaced by an alternative strategy.

The IRA's recognition of futile stalemate, and its consequent preparedness to explore possible political alternatives as a means of struggle, formed the necessary (though not in itself sufficient) foundation on which the subsequent Northern Ireland Peace Process could be built. By 1986 Gerry Adams had acknowledged the reality of 'a situation of deadlock in which Óglaigh na hÉireann [the IRA] were able to block the imposition of a British solution but were unable to force the British to withdraw'.[48] By 1990, this military stalemate was being very clearly noted by other sharp-eyed republicans,[49] and even in 1989 a leading Belfast IRA figure was referring to Martin McGuinness and others talking about 'bringing the armed struggle to a conclusion'.[50] Adams himself had apparently been in indirect dialogue with British politicians during 1986–7, and the implication of all this is of the highest importance in our understanding of how terrorism can, on occasion, come to an end. Provisional IRA violence had emphatically political roots and aims and—potentially—resolution; those involved were as normal and rational as other political actors tend to be, and when years of struggle had taught the lesson that violence was bringing, not the anticipated victory, but instead merely pointless stalemate, then such people looked for alternative ways of achieving political momentum.

This, despite the depressing length of time it took for the futility of violence on all sides to become sufficiently apparent, might be seen as a reasonably encouraging lesson; and it fits perfectly with our established definition and explanatory framework for terrorism. When those involved in terrorist violence recognized that they had potentially more to gain from non-violent than from violent politics, they eschewed the latter in favour of the former.

How could Irish republicans best achieve political leverage, a redress of power relations, and the like? By the end of the 1980s and beginning of the 1990s, they thought that politics rather than violence might provide the answer. This is the essence of explaining the momentous IRA ceasefires of the 1990s, and Irish republicans have been lucid enough on the point. 'The IRA is a very political organization, and it made political decisions on the basis of what it felt it could prosecute.'[51] 'Our [republicans'] sense of it was: how do you keep moving a struggle forward?'[52] 'The IRA stopped because people put a political analysis to them which in their judgment was a project worthy of support.'[53]

Clearly, the republican sea-change in opinion did not occur in isolation from other actors and factors, and some of these had an international dimension. The distinctive 1990s engagement with Northern Ireland by the Clinton regime in Washington added impetus towards a fruitful peace process (especially as it reassured Irish republicans that there was someone involved in the initiative who was more powerful than the British and who was, if anything, sympathetic to nationalist rather than unionist politics in Ireland). The harmonious relationship of British and Irish politicians and civil servants within a European Union context facilitated a joint London–Dublin approach to the North of Ireland, in ways which offered a comparatively reassuring and consistent framework for political negotiations and processes. Again, for those republicans whose struggle had involved a hard-leftist commitment to destroying capitalism, the death of communism closed off expected revolutionary progress and made compromise seem more sensible.[54] (Later on, the impulsion towards abandoning terrorism was strengthened by the effects of 9/11, after which atrocity it was more difficult to imagine the successful sustenance of an IRA-style campaign.[55])

Closer to home, the initiatives of politicians, clergy, and others in opening lines of dialogue with paramilitaries and their political representatives undoubtedly allowed for the exploration of political possibility beyond the bomb and the bullet. In particular, perhaps, the role of constitutional Irish nationalist John Hume of the SDLP deserves mention, as a result of his ongoing and crucial discussions with Sinn Féin leader Gerry Adams. British Secretary of State for Northern Ireland after 1997, Mo Mowlam, later observed that 'The important start to the peace process, talking with Sinn Féin, was achieved by John [Hume]. He took a lot of criticism for it, but it was his work and his vision which made the later progress possible.'[56]

Yet the key foundation on which the Northern Ireland Peace Process was built was the change in strategy by the Provisional IRA, from armed struggle to an essentially non-violent form of politics. And the main reasons for this shift lay in three interlinked changes of perspective on its part, concerning the inefficacy of continued violence, the potential rewards of more peaceful tactics, and the acknowledgement of previously unrecognized political and economic realities.

Just as in the conclusion to an earlier IRA campaign of violence in 1921—though, regrettably, only after a much longer period of killing—blood-spattered stalemate was the condition upon which an end to hostilities was ultimately based. By 1989–90 it was clear (and acknowledged by the British themselves) that the IRA could not be simply militarily defeated; but nor could the forces of the British state or, indeed, those of paramilitary loyalism. There were, in effect, mutually cancelling forms of Clausewitzean pressure being applied to London. Republicans aimed to make the British experience of the Irish war more painful than it would be for London to yield to republican demands; but loyalist violence (and its implied acceleration were Britain indeed to yield to IRA demands) effectively negated the advantage of London so acceding to republican pressure.

Crucial here was the fact that the primary obstacle to British withdrawal from Northern Ireland was not the self-interested engagement of a colonial state, but rather an appreciation that withdrawal was impossible, given the attitudes of the majority of people in Northern Ireland and their undoubted resolve not to be expelled from the UK. In this setting, the logic of IRA violence was the opposite of that assumed by traditional Provo strategy. The Provisionals had pinned their hopes on violence having a cumulatively unbearable quality to it: eventually, the will of the British to remain in the North would be broken by the year-on-year armed struggle. In fact, it is probably nearer the mark to say that, the longer IRA violence continued without producing that result, the more bearable it seemed to a state which had managed to endure it unyieldingly for decades. Put even more sharply, during 1972–6 the IRA killed 722 people, an average of 144 deaths each year; in the entire 1977–2001 period, it never succeeded in killing even a hundred people in any one year. If the British could endure the IRA's lethal activities of 1972–6, would the increasingly lower levels of fatal activity really be likely to produce a more effective republican outcome?

Part of this shift lay in the increasing effectiveness of state counterterrorism. The latter should not be overstated: even at the end of their campaign, the IRA was still in a position to achieve huge and damaging bombings in Britain as well as fatal attacks in Northern Ireland itself. But the latter years of the Provisionals' war were ones during which their ranks were riddled with agents and informers,[57] and this did help to limit their capacity. Amid the revelations of such extensive state penetration, it at times almost seemed as though the IRA's experience echoed G. K. Chesterton's 1908 novel *The Man Who Was Thursday*, in which all seven members of the General Council of an anarchist terrorist group turn out, to each other's surprise, to have been simultaneously working for the police (' "There never was any Supreme Anarchist Council," he said. "We were all a lot of silly policemen looking at each other."... "We are all spies!" '58). Certainly, one lesson from Northern Ireland seems to be that accurate intelligence was of far greater benefit in the fight against terrorism than was the more formal military muscle of, say, the Parachute Regiment.

There were in the late 1980s significant problems with the IRA's military campaign, in terms of the relatively high number of their members being lost in violent action, in terms of the counter-productive IRA killing of manifestly innocent civilians, and in terms also of significant weapons finds by the counter-terrorist authorities. Moreover, the assumed leverage of IRA violence did not seem to be functioning as anticipated. Attacks in England, for example, had been intended to accentuate the immediacy of pressure upon the people there as a way of coercing the London government through popular clamour. But the most thorough account to date of the Provisionals' English bombing campaign concludes that 'While the organization may have achieved significant publicity as a result of their actions in England, there is much evidence to suggest that their impact on British public opinion and British government policy was minimal.'59 Despite bombs in London, Birmingham, Guildford, Brighton, Warrington, and Manchester, the North of Ireland never sustainedly engaged British public or political opinion in such a way as to provide the change in British policy which was sought by the IRA. And I think there's a broader lesson here: bombs did gen-erate great publicity, but they could not provide ultimate resolution of the political conflicts which had prompted them; tenacious and dedicated bombers could sustain a campaign for a long time, but without achieving what their violence was supposed to achieve.

If the acknowledged inefficacy of continued violence represented the first reason for the IRA moving towards a dramatic change of perspective, then the potential reward available from more peace-ful tactics was the second. Here (and again there are surely lessons for our wider response to terrorism), one important element was the ongoing line of communication between the Provisionals and their British opponents. It was in the interests of London to spell out how much benefit would be gained by republicans if only their violence would cease, and this point was repeatedly made over the latter years of the Northern Ireland conflict. (During the early 1990s the Provos were frequently briefed by the British as to government policy, and were even given advance notice of major speeches to be made by British politicians.) What would those rewards and benefits involve? There would be the end to political ghettoization for militant republicans; the prospect of significant reform in the North, concerning matters of central importance such as the police force, for example; prisoner release for incarcerated paramilitaries; the likelihood of far more people voting for Sinn Féin than would ever be the sustained case during an IRA campaign of killing; the consequent possibility of being involved in government both North and South in Ireland; the attractive prospect of wrong-footing unionist opponents, who would find peace more difficult to handle than conflict, and whose case would be more difficult to make to a wider public were the IRA villain to leave the stage. With their violent campaign rather stalled and yielding no further clear momentum, these prospective rewards from peace suggested that the pendulum of effort within the republican movement might more fruitfully swing from the IRA towards its political *alter ego*, Sinn Féin, and this is exactly what occurred. In the end, it was after they had ended their violent campaign that republicans in Northern Ireland came to enjoy their most powerful period of political influence and support.

This process was aided decisively by a third element, and again it is one which follows directly from our recognition that terrorism is only explained as the action chosen by people whose rationality is normal and practical. For republicans by the late 1980s and early 1990s had come to recognize some key political realities which had previously escaped their vision, and—having done so—they pragmatically adjusted their politics and strategy accordingly, with a view to maximizing the benefit that they could gain. There is considerable evidence to suggest that sharp-sighted republicans came by the early 1990s to acknowledge that their reading of Ulster's unionists had been simplistic and naïve. 'In a way we made them a non-people. We just said: you can't move the unionists until you move the Brits. So we didn't even see them as part of the problem, never mind as being part of the solution.'[60] 'When you're engaged in a struggle, you fight with basics in mind. It's a united Ireland or nothing; the unionists are basically tools of British imperialism; they don't know what they're doing; they'll come into a united Ireland like sheep once you break the will of the British. That was a very simplistic view of unionism.'[61] Once unionist views are placed more centrally within view, and unionist opposition to a united Ireland is seen as an enduring obstacle to IRA victory, then more subtle ways of dealing with the problem might seem to be necessitated than had traditionally been involved in IRA thinking and practice.

Similarly, it was recognized that prompt British withdrawal from the North—something long demanded by the Provos—would in fact have catastrophic economic consequences for a region so propped up by British state subvention. Yet again, the legitimacy of the twenty-six-county state in the South in the eyes of its own inhabitants meant that a longer-term approach to reunification might be required, rather than a crude idea of replacing two illegitimate states with one smoothly acquired united Irish republic. Most decisively of all, perhaps, it became clear that the main obstacles to achieving Irish unity lay not in London, but rather in the complex range of views in Ireland itself, North and South. With unionist recalcitrance, with obdurate loyalist resistance, and with southern electorates and governments which were markedly ambivalent about the prospect of unity anyway, the feasibility of the IRA's traditional goal now seemed questionable.[62]

So in Northern Ireland it was not that a prior peace process addressed the root causes of the conflict and then terrorism ended, but rather that the key terrorist movement recognized that its violence was not producing what it had expected it to produce, that there might be greater rewards from peaceful politics, and that political realities demanded a rethinking of strategy. This sea-change decisively allowed for the construction of a peace process which could address some of the root causes of the conflict in ways which allowed for the prospect of sustainable peace in the North of Ireland.

1. & 2. 11th September 2001.

3. 9/11 Conspirator Mohammed Atta.

4. US President George W. Bush speaking in West Virginia about the War on Terror, 2006.

5. Abu Ghraib prison.

6. Aftermath of an ETA car bomb at Madrid airport, January 2007.

7. The Grand Hotel, Brighton, after the IRA's 1984 bomb during the Conservative Party Conference.

8. (*right*) Belfast loyalist mural, 1994.

9. (*below*) British Muslim suicide bombers Omar Khan Sharif and Ashif Muhammad Hanif, Gaza Strip.

10. Hezbollah leader, Hassan Nasrallah.

11. The Alfred P. Murrah Federal Building, Oklahoma City, after the 1995 truck bomb destroyed it.

12. (*left*) The 7/7 bombings, London, 2005.

13. (*below*) Ulrike Meinhof, 1934-76.

14. Osama bin Laden, 2001.

15. British and American hostages, Iraq, 2004.

The deal which emerged was one which took lengthy and difficult work both to construct and then to implement. After protracted talks involving many parties, there emerged on 10 April 1998 the Belfast (or Good Friday) Agreement. This included something to annoy everyone. But it was constructed to offer reassurances and concessions to enough actors in the Northern Ireland conflict for it to become the basis for a lasting peace. The Agreement balanced a respect for the right of the majority within Northern Ireland to remain within the UK, with a recognition of the validity and long-term possibility inherent within Irish nationalists' aspiration towards an independent and united Ireland. Self-determination—a key feature of nationalist argument for many years—was placed at the heart of the deal, but it was to be exercised consensually and within the two respective Irish jurisdictions (North and South), thereby offering reassurance to unionists in Northern Ireland. A Northern Ireland Assembly and Executive were to be established; there were to be both North–South and East–West dimensions embodied in formal councils; commitments were made regarding police reform, prisoner release, equality, human rights, and the decommissioning of paramilitary weapons.

This ambiguous and impressive deal was sold to the rival sides on differing terms. Republicans tended to present it as transitional towards a united Ireland, while its unionist supporters interpreted the Belfast Agreement as a firm barrier against any such development. Each side could see the other as having moved further than it would have preferred (a crucial aspect of the deal's ingenuity), and in referendums held North and South in Ireland on 22 May 1998 there were impressive majorities in favour of supporting it. In the North there was an 81 per cent turn-out, with 71 per cent voting 'Yes' and 29 per cent voting 'No'; a much lower turn-out in the South saw an even clearer margin of victory, with a 'Yes' vote of 94 per cent.

There was then a painfully slow decade between this May 1998 endorsement of the previous month's Agreement and the eventual emergence of an effective Democratic Unionist Party (DUP) / Sinn Féin deal in 2007. Each side tended to mistrust the other's honest commitment to implementing its part of the new order; the slowness of paramilitary (especially IRA) decommissioning and the ongoing levels of paramilitary violence at times threatened to undermine the process altogether; and support for the Agreement within the unionist community slipped as the latter increasingly came to see the Peace Process as one which benefited nationalists to an unfair degree. But in May 2007 the Revd Ian Paisley (DUP leader and long-time anti-republican) became Northern Ireland's First Minister, with Martin McGuinness (leading Sinn Féiner and a former IRA leader) as his Deputy First Minister in a Belfast power-sharing administration. This was an extraordinarily striking arrangement: as Tony Blair's chief negotiator, Jonathan Powell, honestly put it, 'If anyone had asked me when I first stepped into Downing Street as Tony Blair's Chief of Staff in May 1997 whether I ever expected to see Ian Paisley and Martin McGuinness sharing power in Stormont I would have thought they were mad.'[63] Paisley and McGuinness would briefly head an Executive whose twelve members were drawn from the four main political parties in Northern Ireland (the DUP, Sinn Féin, the SDLP, and the Ulster Unionist Party (UUP)). This Executive, comprising former enemies working in comparative harmony, was then linked to the 108-member Assembly which had been set up under the 1998 Belfast Agreement.

Central to the creation of this fragile new order in Northern Ireland was the sense, outlined above, that violence had led to long-term stalemate rather than offering any realistic prospect of victory. But that in itself would not be enough to produce something like genuine peace. For the latter, what was also required was a shared sense of political legitimacy for the state and the political arrangement within it. Establishing a polity which commanded effective support and which was considered legitimate by an effective majority of the community: this was what had undermined the old IRA after 1922 within independent Ireland, and this was the hope in the very different circumstances of the North at the end of the twentieth and beginning of the twenty-first century. In each of these epochal cases, an appeal to the pragmatism of those who had been involved in prior violence and militancy was essential and, ultimately, effective. In the 1920s, Irish nationalists Michael Collins and (more belatedly) Eamon de Valera recognized the realities of power sufficiently to accept the substantial compromises being made by their opponents; in the 1990s and beyond, a similar process seems to have carried people like Gerry Adams and Martin McGuinness from aggressive Provisionalism to a more measured and constitutional form of politics.

In the modern-day Northern Irish case—as, again, in earlier phases of Irish republican history—the question of leadership was vitally important. No deal will satisfy all. But if there does appear the prospect of establishing a mutually respected state legitimacy within which political rivals can peacefully and successfully participate, then it is crucial that leaders can manage the shift towards such a new order while bringing enough of their people along with them. In particular, this is vital in regard to those sections of the community which, rightly or wrongly, had previously rejected the state's very legitimacy, but who might now come to recognize it.

A part of this which again possesses some possible wider lessons is that power will come to be held by some whose past actions make that a difficult sight for many to witness. Those in power in 1920s and 1930s independent Ireland frequently had bloodstained hands from earlier phases of the struggle.[64] In twenty-first-century Ulster, unionists had to stomach the prospect of an ex-IRA man as their Deputy First Minister and of a government within which much power was wielded by the IRA's political party. For those who had not shared Sinn Féin leader Gerry Adams's (and his party's) view that IRA violence was 'a necessary and morally correct form of resistance'[65] within Northern Ireland, this was a difficult reality to face.

With the Provisional IRA's political party enjoying shared governmental power in the new Northern Ireland, should we derive the lesson that terrorism works? Opinions vary starkly on what should be learned here.[66] But some important points need to be established. The first aim of terrorist organizations is merely to endure, and the Provisionals impressively managed this over several decades and despite the enormous resources that were arrayed against them by the UK (and, indeed, the Irish) state. Moreover, their violence did alter the power relations between the Catholic community which they claimed to represent in the North and the UK state against which the IRA was campaigning. This was true during their pre-ceasefire violence. But it was also evident during the ensuing Peace Process and negotiations, when the threat of IRA violence was used as a means of exerting greater republican leverage over Britain. Furthermore, it had long been an argument proffered by the republican movement that all gains or concessions enjoyed in Northern Ireland by the nationalist minority should be seen as having been produced by the IRA: it was, they claimed, only because of the IRA's violence that the British would yield such ground at all. Yet again, the IRA's violence did make the issue of Irish self-determination a matter of much greater international note and prominence.

On the other hand, if one examines what the Provisional IRA itself actually sought to achieve during its war, it becomes clear that most of these objectives were left substantially unrealized at the end of its campaign. Its violence was strategic, aimed at the achievement of key goals, and deployed because only that violence was deemed effective in pursuing them: so it is important to ask, to what extent had these central goals been achieved? The Provos had emerged partly because of a perceived need to defend Catholic communities from violent attack. Could they, in fact, do this? Largely, the answer has to be that they could not. As we have already seen, IRA violence could at times prompt increased rather than diminished likelihood of murderous loyalist assault on Catholic victims. And while Gerry Adams has argued that by 1972 the Provisional IRA had 'created a defensive force of unprecedented effectiveness',[67] this is a view which conflicts with the evidence. Despite some courageous episodes, it remains hard to sustain the argument that the IRA was an effective defender of the northern Catholic community during these early days of the Troubles. During the first three years of the Provisionals' existence (from 18 December 1969 to 17 December 1972), 171 Catholic civilians were killed by loyalists or the security forces. Indeed, it is sadly more plausible to argue that, during the

Troubles as a whole, IRA violence made more rather than less likely the prospect of Catholics suffering violence.[68]

More central even than defence, however, was the IRA's aim of realizing Irish national self-determination, understood as properly embodied in the sovereignty and unity of a fully independent, thirty-two-county Irish republic. The IRA long interpreted self-determination as rightfully involving the will of the people of Ireland acting as a single unit, rather than in two partitioned entities (since it considered the Northern Irish unionist majority to represent an illegitimate veto over Irish national self-determination itself). The armed struggle was engaged in with an explicitly expressed view to achieving complete British withdrawal from Ireland and the establishment of complete, all-Ireland sovereignty: 'there is but one solution and that solution is based upon British disengagement';[69] 'Outside of a thirty-two-county sovereign, independent democracy the IRA will have no involvement in what is loosely called constitutional politics.'[70]

But the ending of British sovereignty over Northern Ireland emphatically did not form part of the 1998 Belfast Agreement; nor does it seem imminent that popular opinion in the North will allow for its emergence. The 2001 Census reported 44 per cent of the people of Northern Ireland to have a Catholic community background, 53 per cent to come from a Protestant community background, and 3 per cent designated as other. Even if this were to change so that over 50 per cent of the population were Catholic, there is no certainty at all of a majority vote in favour of a united Ireland, a point reinforced by the fact that only 50 per cent even of nationalist SDLP members themselves declare a united Ireland to be the best solution for the North.[71] And of course there would—even in the event of a northern majority in favour of British withdrawal—be the obstacles, first, of attitudes within an ambivalent Republic of Ireland and, second, of a sizeable number of unionists and loyalists who might resist incorporation into a united Ireland by force, just as the IRA had violently resisted membership of the UK in the past.

If neither defence nor Irish unity were brought about by the IRA's armed struggle, then nor were some other significant goals to which they had repeatedly proclaimed commitment, whether the establishment of Irish socialism (Martin McGuinness: 'We are a socialist republican movement, a movement that supports the use of armed struggle in the six counties and the establishment of a socialist republic in the thirty-two counties of Ireland'[72]), or the ending of Irish sectarianism. The IRA had seen the latter as having originated with the English and having been sustained by Protestant forces:

> Who started sectarianism? The English murderers who invaded Ireland, massacred the native population who were Catholic and established a Protestant Ascendancy based on the Penal Laws and backed by all the forces of the British Empire. Who maintained sectarianism? First the English and Scottish landlords and later the Protestant working class and planters, through the Orange Order, by discrimination, corruption, and terrorism.[73]

Quite rightly, Irish republicans have condemned the sectarianism practised by their opponents. But the reality of the Provisional IRA's own violence was that it, along with that of others in the conflict, tended to reinforce sectarian polarization and division. The Northern Ireland system in which Martin McGuinness was to inherit such a prominent part in 2007 was one dominated by two political parties—Sinn Féin and the DUP—each of which enjoyed virtually no support whatever from the other confessional community, and by this stage Troubles violence had deepened rather than dissolved the sharpness of this division between the two communities.

Does terrorism work? The answer from the case of the Provisional IRA is not, I think, entirely clear-cut. But it *is* evident from this case study that violence has the capacity to make an important political problem seem far more urgent of redress, while also contributing to that lack of trust which hampers eventual resolution of the same problem. IRA violence did change the world, and its supporters would claim that only its actions prompted the reforms which were eventually brought about in the 1998 deal and beyond. But in terms of the central goals for which the IRA was fighting at the time of its campaign—British withdrawal, Irish unity, defence of

Catholic communities from violence, socialism—it is clear that the Provisionals' campaign was far from effective, as judged against the outcome emerging in the first decade of the twenty-first century.

This is not to belittle the seriousness of the IRA's grievances, its commitment, or the fact that its violence did have some strong impact. In a straightforward military sense, the IRA did not lose: it had the capacity to continue with its campaign, and it could ensure that the British did not impose things without its own endorsement. But what it—the Provisional IRA—eventually settled for in the North of Ireland was far, far less than it had been fighting for, and in this sense its violence must be judged ultimately to have been profoundly ineffective.

II

To what extent might these Irish lessons, drawn particularly from the case of the Provisional IRA, illuminate our reading of the wider history of terrorism?

Why do significant terrorist campaigns begin? In our arguments regarding definition and explanation, and in their application to the Irish case study, we have seen the following: the vital importance of disaggregation into specific geographical and political settings, combined with a recognition of the often long-rooted history involved in relevant conflict; the frequency with which issues of contested political legitimacy lie at the heart of eruptions of terrorism, especially when these include matters surrounding religiously inflected nationalisms in competition with one another, the mismatch between nation and state, and problems of self-determination and political boundaries; the intensifying role which the experience of day-to-day unfairness for a population plays in preparing people to engage in or to tolerate terrorist violence as a response; the sense that violence represents a strategically necessary means of achieving justified and essential goals, a psychologically rewarding method of hitting back in reaction to prior violence, and an effective way of redressing unfair power imbalances currently in existence; the importance in many cases of foreign occupation of one's territory and of friction between military enemies and one's fellow civilians in the occupied area; the resources offered by ideological tradition and argument, as a means of explaining an emerging crisis and justifying terrorist response to it; and the interweaving of political with cultural and religious and economic experience.

It is not possible simply to export Irish lessons around the rest of the planet. But it could be argued that much of what has just been established also possesses profound importance for our understanding of terrorism in many settings. Certainly, the importance of locally rooted analysis and explanation is crucial.[74] And when we examine important cases of terrorist violence within local contexts of politics and struggle, we see many of the above themes evident in the story of why violence erupts. What we designate terrorist crises often enough revolve around long-rooted issues of nationalism, sovereignty, and self-determination, whether in Ireland, Lebanon,[75] Palestine, Chechnya, or many other places. The case of the Basque group ETA illustrates the point reasonably well. Founded in 1959, ETA believes that the Basque country[76] requires national sovereignty as the necessary means of preserving its cultural heritage and ancestral language. The struggle here between regionalism and centralism in Spain undoubtedly has very long historical roots, and involves a profound intersection of politics with culture. The long roots can be seen in the persistent Basque sense—both in Spain and in France—that theirs has been a history of nation without state (authority having long resided with the Spanish and French states instead). France enjoyed only partial success in the nineteenth century in absorbing and integrating Basques into Frenchness, while the same century witnessed Basques also offering some resistance to the centralizing initiatives of the Spanish state. Formal Basque party politics has an impressively lengthy history, going back to the nineteenth century, and in the Spanish case especially there has persisted a strong sense of defiant non-incorporation into the wider state.

A vital aspect of this involved distinctive Basque culture: many Basques not only speak Euskera, but see it as interwoven with their own distinctive identity. And Basque language, customs, and belief in a shared historical culture have all reinforced an emphasis on the distinctiveness of Basque identity and the legitimacy, therefore, of political separation. Other cultural elements have also strengthened Basque community: although the past generation has seen the Catholic dimension to Basque nationalism greatly diminish, it was long true in both Hegoalde and Iparralde that the Catholic Church played a significant role in defending and promoting Basque culture; and for many people and for many years Catholicism represented an important strand within Basque identity.

As with so many other violent nationalist groups, so also with ETA, it would be wrong to confuse their claim to represent the whole nation with universal support for their actions and politics. ETA's political wing was renamed in 2001 as Batasuna (Unity); in its earlier guise, as Herri Batasuna (People's Unity), the party frequently polled between 15 and 20 per cent in Basque elections, reflecting the fact that most people in Hegoalde were not supportive of Basque violence. Despite the headline-wresting activities of ETA, it was the moderate Basque nationalist party—PNV (Partido Nacionalista Vasco)—which tended to be the dominant force in recent Basque nationalism in terms of votes. During the post-Franco period there has emerged notable autonomy for the Basque region within the Spanish state; and at the first autonomous regional election held in 1980, within Basque Spain the PNV won 38 per cent of the vote, with Herri Batasuna managing only 16 per cent. This pattern has tended to persist: in the 1996 Spanish elections, for example, the PNV won 26 per cent of the vote to Herri Batasuna's 13 per cent.

The pattern here, therefore, is one of zealous separatists, whose militancy is supported by a significant minority of a constituent population. And while it is important to recognize the majority opinion against their violent politics, it is also crucial in our explanation of the emergence of serious terrorism that there is a significant section of the people who endorse such a violent approach. Moreover, while ETA's violent version of Basque separatism has not enjoyed anything like universal support in the region, it remains clear that some of its aims do resonate reasonably widely, and that the group's essential sanity and normality are generally recognized. An opinion poll from November 1979, for example, showed that 54 per cent of Basques considered ETA to be 'patriots or idealists', while only 14 per cent thought them 'madmen or criminals'.[77]

So this Basque historical case reflects our wider pattern of explanation, with sustained terrorism emerging in a deep-rooted setting of contested legitimacy; with the politics of nation-versus-state and of problematic self-determination; with a religiously and culturally inflected and embedded nationalism; with a perceived need for violence as a means of achieving leverage and the redress of unbalanced power relations; and with violence seeming more legitimate against the background of grievances born of day-to-day experience (that of the Basque community under Franco, for instance).

But does a similar pattern emerge when we consider the most famous and, to some in the West, the most bafflingly exotic of modern terrorisms, that of al-Qaeda and its Islamist associates?

As we have noted, the emergence of al-Qaeda can be adequately explained only within a particular time and place: the response of some Muslims to political events in Afghanistan under Soviet rule, and the subsequent trajectory of Saudi Arabian relations with the United States. And while there remains much that is still unknown about this transnational network, there is little doubt about the political goals and rationale centrally involved, and it might be worth looking in more detail at the historical case study in this light. The policy demands of Osama bin Laden are reasonably straightforward (however misjudged or unrealistic): to communicate to the United States through violence, for example, the high cost of maintaining unpopular US foreign policy in the Muslim world; to remove American troops from Saudi Arabia; to limit Washington's support for certain pro-Western rulers in Muslim countries, and for Israel; and so on. And the roots and development of al-Qaeda also exemplify our argument that terrorism—however repellent—lies well within the range of rational political explanation, when seen in historical context and understood in its varying phases.

Al-Qaeda emerged initially as a function of the anti-Soviet war in Afghanistan, and as such it was a recognizable product of the

Cold War. Born in 1988—as al-Qaeda al-Sulbah (the solid base)—its decisive first creator was Abdullah Azzam, the key ideologue behind the anti-Soviet war in Afghanistan and a Jordanian-Palestinian cleric from the West Bank. Al-Qaeda's origins were as a group supporting those Arabs who went to Afghanistan to fight against the Soviets; but Azzam's view of al-Qaeda's mission was that it would channel the energies of the mujahidin into fighting on behalf of oppressed Muslims wherever they were in the world.

Osama bin Laden was Azzam's protégé, and it was bin Laden who formally established al-Qaeda as an organization in Pakistan in August 1988, partly with a view to continuing the jihad beyond its Afghan theatre. The following year saw bin Laden and Azzam split from one another regarding al-Qaeda's appropriate priorities, and Azzam himself was assassinated in Pakistan in November 1989 by members of the Egyptian group Islamic Jihad, apparently with bin Laden's acquiescence.

When the Soviets withdrew from Afghanistan in 1989, al-Qaeda duly began to aid local jihadist movements in various countries (Algeria, Chechnya, Bosnia, and Egypt included) in their respective struggles against perceivedly unwelcome governments. It is known that during 1989–2001 Afghanistan was a vital haven for al-Qaeda, which appears to have trained thousands of jihadists there. But again this fits a broader political framework, with the 1989–2001 period having been designated, for example, by the influential commentator Walter Russell Mead as 'lost years in American foreign policy. From November 9, 1989, when the Berlin Wall came down, through September 11, 2001, three administrations from two parties beguiled themselves with pleasing illusions about the health of the American system even as formidable challenges to that system were assembling offshore.'[78] The al-Qaeda/Afghan story fits this pattern dismally, representing as it did a sharp and lethal example of the gathering mood among some Muslims of aggressive hostility towards the United States.

When, after the Soviet withdrawal from Afghanistan, Osama bin Laden went to Saudi Arabia, he was enraged by the presence of US troops there as part of Operation Desert Shield in 1990, and by their continuing presence after the Gulf War. It was this—a response to unwelcome foreign military occupation of precious territory —which led him to campaign against the Saudi regime, and to demand that what he saw as a falsely Muslim al-Saud authority be replaced with a truly Islamic regime and state—again, in itself an entirely recognizable politics of ideologically driven pursuit of state regime change.

Having fallen out with the Saudi authorities, bin Laden based himself during 1991–6 in Sudan. In May of 1996 he left Khartoum and returned to Jalalabad, Afghanistan. At this point, significantly, Western intelligence agencies had virtually no presence in Afghanistan, and so al-Qaeda was able to reorganize, train, and grow stronger, with the West having lost track of it. Having been something of a hero in the anti-Soviet struggle, bin Laden was warmly welcomed back to Afghanistan (again, the politics of resisting foreign military occupation were crucial here), and he aimed from his Afghan base to set up a genuinely global jihadist network. During the final years of the twentieth century Afghanistan therefore became the centre for al-Qaeda operations and training, and the shocking atrocity of 11 September 2001 flowed from this sequence of events: 'From Afghanistan bin Laden directed a number of terrorist operations that included the 1998 bombings of the US embassies in Kenya and Tanzania, the October 2000 attack on the USS Cole, and the 9/11 attacks on New York and Washington. Bin Laden's safe haven in Afghanistan ultimately allowed him to finance and support numerous jihadist organizations worldwide.'[79]

In explaining how, historically, serious terrorism has emerged, the case of 9/11 itself obviously cannot be ignored. Some have seen the event in epoch-defining terms, as changing the world and inaugurating a newly defining conflict against Islamist terrorists. In Martin Amis's words, 'September 11 has given to us a planet we barely recognize';[80] according to Fred Halliday, 'The crisis unleashed by the events of 11 September is one that is global and all-encompassing. It is global in the sense that it binds many different countries into conflict, most obviously the USA and parts of the Muslim world. It is all-encompassing in that, more than any other international crisis yet seen, it affects a multiplicity of life's levels, political, economic, cultural and psychological.'[81]

The nineteen martyrs who carried out the 9/11 attacks subsequently came to be celebrated by jihadists as hugely significant heroes of the Islamist cause—the expectation of glorification cannot be discounted in our explanation of why they did as they did—and there is no doubt about the giant scale of the effect of their bloody gesture. The attacks of September 2001 killed nearly 3,000 people drawn from many countries, and so in one combined assault they killed more people than had died in the previous decade from international terrorism; the terrifying attacks, repeatedly transmitted around the world on television screens, became globally visible and extraordinary in their iconic significance. By causing huge destruction in New York, Washington, and Pennsylvania, 9/11 hit the United States at home in a novel version of international terrorist activity, and this possessed huge psychological effect, making the USA feel unprecedentedly vulnerable to massive domestic terrorist attack. So terrorism became a shared, major priority, in a way that it had not been seen in the very early stages of George W. Bush's presidency (despite warnings at the start of 2001 from people like White House counter-terrorism specialist Richard Clarke—former head of counter-terrorism under Bill Clinton and George W. Bush—that 'al-Qaeda is at war with us, it is a highly capable organization, probably with sleeper cells in the US, and it is clearly planning a major series of attacks against us'[82]).

It could, perhaps, be countered that the world-changing effects of 9/11 have been exaggerated. This was not the first attack on New York's World Trade Center by people linked to Osama bin Laden, and the 26 February 1993 attack (which had killed six and injured more than a thousand) might very easily have had much larger consequences and presumably was intended to do so: had there been more explosives involved, and had the truck containing them been differently situated, then a far more catastrophic outcome might have resulted. And there was certainly nothing new about terrorist attacks against US-related targets as such. Since the late 1960s it has been the United States that has been the most frequently targeted victim of terrorist attacks (albeit usually US people and property, but not normally on US soil).[83] Nor was there anything particularly new about attacks focusing on the aviation industry: since the 1960s this has been a very common mode of attack, the hijacking of planes for terrorist effect being highly familiar.[84] And even in terms of the USA responding to Islamist attack as having initiated a war, there were pre-9/11 resonances. After attacks on US embassies in Africa in 1998, United States Secretary of State Madeleine Albright had declared that America was at war with religious terrorists: this was, she said, 'the war of the future' and would involve a 'long-term struggle'.[85]

But, for our purposes here, it is less important to recognize that 9/11 brought change while leaving much unaltered, than to remember the event in terms of explaining why it occurred. And here, again, we see a very recognizable and even rational set of elements. Osama bin Laden had witnessed the vulnerability of one perceivedly anti-Muslim superpower, and he now felt that another was equally vulnerable and deserving of attack. Even if the strategic rationale here was faulty (and it almost certainly was), it is clear that there was a strategic argument and assessment at the heart of the scheme. This was a war against the American-led West: bin Laden had expressly declared it as such, and his military operational commander Khalid Sheikh Mohammed (alias 'Mokhtar' or 'The Brain', and allegedly the mastermind planner of the 9/11 operation) likewise saw himself very much at war with the United States.

And this was a war supposedly justified by prior crimes, including those related to foreign military occupation (Saudi Arabia),[86] contested state legitimacy and self-determination (Israel/Palestine), and the need to alter power relations in terms of state regime and authority (Saudi Arabia, Egypt, Chechnya, the Philippines). If bin Laden could provoke and bait the USA into costly wars throughout the Islamic world, might he help to bankrupt the United States as he had helped to bankrupt the Soviet Union beforehand?

It is hard to be precise in our explanation of precisely why bin Laden's passions developed in this direction (Martin Amis has mischievously observed that he found himself 'frivolously wondering

whether Osama was just the product of his family background—
and more particularly of his birth order. Seventeenth out of fifty-
seven is a notoriously difficult slot to fill'[87]). But it is clear that
strong ideological influence had an impact: as a student at Jeddah's
King Abdul Aziz University, he came under the important influence of Islamists such as Muhammad Qutb—brother of Sayyid—
and Abdullah Azzam. And this ideological framework supported a
violent politics which is not, in itself, beyond rational comprehension. Why carry out the 9/11 attacks? Bin Laden's own justification
was clear enough:

> The United States and their allies are killing us in Palestine, Chech-
> nya, Kashmir and Iraq. That's why Muslims have the right to carry out
> revenge attacks on the US.... The American people should remem-
> ber that they pay taxes to their government and that they voted for
> their president. Their government makes weapons and provides them
> to Israel, which they use to kill Palestinian Muslims. Given that the
> American Congress is a committee that represents the people, the fact
> that it agrees with the actions of the American government proves
> that America in its entirety is responsible for the atrocities that it is
> committing against Muslims. I demand the American people to take
> note of their government's policy against Muslims.... The onus is on
> Americans to prevent Muslims from being killed at the hands of their
> government.[88]

So when we properly remember 9/11, the psychological—the
question of revenge and hatred and of hitting back[89]—yet again
coalesces with political-strategic aspects as we produce an explanation of terrorism. It's not that prior violence by an enemy state
legitimates the kind of atrocity practised in 2001. Even if one did
suppose US actions to be repressive and harsh, this cannot blind us
to the hideous futility of the 9/11 attacks. (Once again, this pattern
of mutual brutality was recognized by Joseph Conrad in his reflections on terror nearly a century ago: 'The ferocity and imbecility
of an autocratic rule rejecting all legality and in fact basing itself
upon complete moral anarchism provokes the no less imbecile and
atrocious answer of a purely Utopian revolutionism encompassing
destruction by the first means to hand, in the strange conviction

that a fundamental change of hearts must follow the downfall of any given human institutions.'[90]) But the supposed inexplicability of an act such as 9/11 results in part from myopia regarding the role of states in generating anti-state violence by their own policies and legacies, and this broad point is now well recognized in the literature on revolutions.[91]

If this is relevant to 9/11, then it is important elsewhere too, and it reflects the central theme of our argument here. In the long-rooted origins of 9/11 there were specific, geographically and politically localized issues of contested state legitimacy and of the mismatch between nation and state; there were ideological resources of some allure and depth, and these seemed to justify a violence which offered both psychological rewards and also a strategically effective and necessary way of redressing power imbalances, foreign occupation, and the day-to-day political, cultural, economic, and religious hardship of one's own community. In its own unique way, 9/11 echoed precisely the same kind of disastrous sequences of political interaction that we can see elsewhere, from Ireland to Palestine to Algeria and Cyprus.

The 9/11 case study in historical memory is also the most obviously compelling as we turn to our second question: *How are terrorist campaigns sustained?* More particularly, in the post-9/11 era we can see a multi-causal process, featuring the self-fuelling dynamics of violence itself (especially, perhaps, the effect of state violence against civilians); the importance of sustained political commitment, tied to a belief in the efficacy of violence; the resonance of such belief with wider sympathies beyond the actual violent organization, and their partial sustenance through the interaction of cultural and religious with political ideas; the importance of some external actors; the sustaining effect of organizational dynamics themselves, including those of non-violent but associated campaigns; and the role of leadership, whether inspiring, influencing, mentoring, intimidating, or directing.

The post-9/11 sequence of international conflict has provided a gruesome illustration of the self-sustaining dynamics of terrorist-related conflict. Much of this has been intricately interwoven with the understandably huge US response to the atrocity of 2001. By the end of June 2002, 1,600 people with alleged al-Qaeda or associated links were being detained in many countries. More broadly, the United States responded with the 'War on Terror' and with more grounded wars in Afghanistan and then in Iraq. In addressing the nation on 11 September 2001 itself, President George W. Bush proclaimed that 'America and our friends and allies join with all those who want peace and security in the world, and we stand together to win the war against terrorism.' Nine days later, the 'War on Terror' was more formally inaugurated. In his address to a joint session of Congress and the US people on 20 September, Bush stated: 'Our war on terror begins with al-Qaeda, but it does not end there. It will not end until every terrorist group of global reach has been found, stopped and defeated.' Later developments, such as the ensuing war in Afghanistan, were set firmly within this orbit: on 29 November 2001, for example, the President declared that 'Afghanistan is the first overseas front in this war against terror'.[92]

It is, of course, understandable and to be expected that the world's single superpower should respond very powerfully to an attack such as that experienced on 11 September; and it's perfectly reasonable that the USA should aim to defend itself and, indeed, to promote peace and democratic stability around the world as a means of doing so. Moreover, in itself there is nothing wrong with recognizing that jihadist terrorists are engaged in a war against the West. The question is whether the precise concept and practice of the American War on Terror have been as effective as they might have been. One can broadly sympathize with the US desire to thwart terrorist violence, while still arguing that many features of recent US foreign policy have, in fact, made things more rather than less difficult.

There are those who have argued that declaring War on Terror was, in a literal sense, missing the point: 'Except as a metaphor, there can be no such thing as a "war against terror" or against terrorism, only against particular political actors who use what is a tactic, not a programme.'[93] And the real test for this new American war was to be found within the two more physical contexts in which the USA became involved: for the War on Terror was to involve a massive militarization of response, in Afghanistan and then in Iraq.

On 7 October 2001 there commenced 'Operation Enduring Freedom', with a US-led coalition invading Afghanistan. This was a direct and speedy response to 9/11: it involved an offensive against the Afghan Taliban regime and its al-Qaeda guests, and it had the clear aims of overthrowing the former and capturing or killing as many as possible of the latter. This was not merely a case of punishing the wrongdoer—though that also played its part, especially given the Taliban's failure to hand over Osama bin Laden and to close al-Qaeda camps in Afghanistan. The idea was also that if one could replace the Taliban with a more moderate and pro-Western regime, then US interests and safety would be better guaranteed; al-Qaeda's safe haven would be closed down, and some sort of hold over the troubled country might be established.

The Taliban regime duly collapsed, with the fall of Kabul in November 2001. The alternative Northern Alliance was put in control of Kabul, and there can be no doubt that the initial overthrow of the Taliban after 9/11 did serious damage to al-Qaeda. In October 2001 it is estimated that there were around 3,000–4,000 members in the core of al-Qaeda; the war in Afghanistan did take to pieces the infrastructure of the group there and remove from them their vital safe location. By 2008, one might even argue that al-Qaeda was less a group than a very loose network of association and attitude, dangerous though this might still prove.

But while the invasion had indeed removed the hated old order, it did not bring stability to the country. Attacks by the Taliban rose from 1,632 in 2005 to 5,388 in 2006, and suicide attacks from 27 in 2005 to 139 in 2006.[94] As late as 2007, fighting was still very fierce in parts of Afghanistan, and it even appeared that, if anything, the insurgency against the new government was growing in strength. Often enough, the use of large-scale military force by an occupying or invading army—especially when it will damage civilian populations—is able to bring ambiguous and at times painful results, and this happened in Afghanistan too. The killing of Afghan civilians by US forces, the repeated house searches and arrests and friction with the military, have tended in places to deepen rather than erase disaffection and hostility. Moreover, the problem of dealing sensitively with the population, and of acquiring and applying detailed intelligence in the Afghan setting, was worsened after 2003 when some of those who were gaining expertise appropriate to Afghanistan were relocated to the other major military theatre of the War on Terror: Iraq.[95]

It's well-recognized that the mobilization of challenges to the state tends to elicit a repressive state response.[96] Indeed, in terms of the dynamics of terrorism, it is the state's response to initial challenge which is often of decisive effect, as a perception that the state is repressing one's own group can prompt a much greater toleration for anti-state terrorism. There can be few more striking cases of this paradoxical symbiosis, achieved between terrorists and their state enemies, than the Iraq War which began in 2003.

The war which commenced on 19 March 2003—'Operation Iraqi Freedom'—involved both aerial bombing and troop invasion, and should be seen within both a longer- and a shorter-term context. In relation to the former, we need to note that well before 9/11 the US administration had had an eye on regime change in Iraq; we should also recognize that the United States had long been prone to the interwoven beliefs that it was an embodiment of freedom within an unfree wider world, and that it was the only agent which could, in fact, bring freedom to the rest of the world. There was a historical self-image of real weight here: 'the self-definition of the United States as a nation-state with a special mission to bring freedom to all mankind'.[97]

Whatever the longer-term perspective, 9/11 was presented by the USA and its allies as justifying this particular delivery of Iraqi freedom, on the dubious grounds of there having been a supposed connection between the regime of Saddam Hussein and the September terrorists. It was also argued (much more plausibly) that Hussein's regime was appallingly brutal, and that there was a legitimate need to liberate the country from his tyranny; and (dubiously again, as it turned out) that Iraq posed a direct and imminent military threat to the West, especially through its alleged possession of

Weapons of Mass Destruction (WMD)—chemical, biological, and nuclear weapons.

Post-9/11, it was understandable for the United States to prioritize its security, but the particular arguments deployed here were not, perhaps, the strongest. It became clear that there had been no evidence linking Hussein to 9/11 (something the Bush administration eventually admitted); the Iraqi leader had indeed offered support to other terrorists, but in this particular case he was not the guilty man. Famously, too, it became clear in time that Hussein had not possessed WMD capacity, and that the imminent threat posed to the West was not as great as had been proclaimed from Washington and London. The third part of the argument—the awfulness of the Iraqi regime—was entirely fair, except that it had not been used consistently by the USA or the UK in relation to awful regimes elsewhere (or even to Saddam's own rule when this had suited Western interests. During the 1980–8 Iran–Iraq War, for example, the USA had seen Hussein as a very useful bulwark against Iran, and had duly supported him).

There probably was a more forceful line of argument available, to the effect that while Saddam did not possess WMD, he clearly wanted to do so; and that a Hobbesian, pre-emptive, defensive strike before he did so made much greater strategic sense than waiting to deal with him when he did possess more dangerous weapons. But this argument lacked the attractive urgency and decisive morality of the three cases that were actually offered. Whatever the reasoning, it is clear that the United States had taken a clear decision— apparently by early 2002[98]—to go to war against Iraq regardless of its allies' views; decisive influences to this effect included Donald Rumsfeld (Secretary of Defense) and Paul Wolfowitz (Deputy Secretary of Defense).

The war was to have complex effects, among which the counterproductive impact of alleged human rights abuses by the USA and its allies famously became significant. Anxiety about the mistreatment of suspects held in the War on Terror went back to the early stages of the Afghan War. But it was the detention centre at the US Naval Base at Guantánamo Bay, Cuba, that established notoriety for this part of the anti-terror struggle. Most of the Guantánamo detainees had been captured in Afghanistan and were treated not as prisoners of war but rather as enemy combatants who could be held indefinitely. During their Cuban stay, they were interrogated by CIA, FBI, and military inquisitors in the understandable pursuit of high-grade intelligence.

This particular detainee question was not, however, especially well handled, and so, not for the first time in the history of counter-terrorism, something of a propaganda and political victory was handed to those against whom the detention had been aimed. During 2002 complaints grew about the treatment of detainees at Guantánamo,[99] and human rights groups began to mount an internationally visible campaign. In particular, it was suggested that the provisions of the Geneva Convention should apply to those who had been captured in Afghanistan. Allied to possibly inhuman and degrading treatment during the interrogation process, there was also the issue of the extent to which the right people had been detained in the first place. And even where the right people had indeed been captured, was it clear that what they told you under duress was accurate and important?

There were voices within the US government and armed forces putting the case against the harsh treatment practised at Guantánamo, but they failed to win the argument, and the result was deeply damaging to the USA's moral reputation abroad. A January 2007 BBC World Service poll of more than 26,000 people across twenty-five countries showed 67 per cent of people disapproving of America's handling of those held at Guantánamo.[100] By late 2004 there were around 600 detainees being held at Guantánamo Bay, and the stories of their maltreatment helped provide some further emotional legitimation for hitting back at the United States (just as the degrading treatment of some of these detainees had itself reflected an American sense of the legitimacy of American hitting back at those perceived to have been supportive of the 9/11 atrocity). Even well into 2008, the retention of more than 240 people at Guantánamo Bay, indefinitely detained without charge, continued publicly to undermine US credibility in the War on Terror.[101]

The issue of prisoner abuse became more problematic still with the publicizing of events in Iraq itself at Abu Ghraib prison, twenty miles west of Baghdad. This had been a notorious jail under Saddam Hussein's brutal regime, and it had now become a US military prison. By the autumn of 2003 there were several thousand prisoners being held there, and by the following year a scandal had developed regarding abuse of those being detained: beatings, sexual humiliations, and other abuses, including the use of unmuzzled dogs to frighten prisoners,[102] again undermined the United States's moral authority in its War on Terror, and generated an international public relations disaster, especially with the widespread dissemination of photographic images of abuse.

In the light of such episodes, it is hardly surprising to find legal scholarship suggesting that prisoner abuse within the War on Terror is likely to mobilize rather than neutralize violent opposition to the states waging that war.[103] And what we see here is a specific, post-9/11 version of the broader pattern by means of which state response to terrorism can, at times, help to sustain that very terrorism which the state quite rightly wants to extirpate. Abuses at Guantánamo Bay and Abu Ghraib are simply not on the same scale of awfulness as the attacks of 9/11. But they do form part of a broader effect which has led many observers to consider that the US War on Terror has made the threat of terrorism rather worse.[104] Certainly, the abrasiveness and insensitivity of the Bush regime have damaged America's image in the wider world, among allies and potential enemies alike, and there is considerable popular, scholarly, and practitioner-generated evidence to support such a claim.

Many young Muslims have been radicalized by the perceived injustice of, in particular, the Iraq War, Iraq now being seen by many radical Islamists as the land of jihad. Moreover, the repercussions of this stretch much further. Members of the terrorist cell convicted in April 2007 of plotting bomb attacks in England clearly had a sense that the UK should be hit expressly because of its support for the US wars in Afghanistan and Iraq.[105] As leading counter-terrorism experts have noted, 'Rather than dissuade potential jihadists from becoming involved in terrorism, the prosecution of the "War on

Terror" in Iraq has had the opposite effect... The worldwide threat of terrorism has increased several-fold since the US invasion of Iraq.'[106]

At the start of 2007 an extensive international poll showed profound disquiet with the American-led War on Terror and US foreign policy, with 73 per cent of people disapproving of the way in which the USA had dealt with Iraq, and 68 per cent thinking that America's military presence in the Middle East provoked more conflict than it prevented.[107] The Iraq mission has damaged international sympathy and support for the USA, from Germany to Russia to France, and from Indonesia to Lebanon to Turkey to Pakistan to Jordan.[108] In particular, US standing in the Muslim world itself has fallen dramatically as a result of Iraq.[109] And since so many Muslims consider the Iraq War to be unjust, it has become more difficult for the USA to sustain a meaningful alliance of forces against terrorism which includes Muslim governments (and, of course, such an alliance is exactly what is most needed).

What Eric Hobsbawm has bluntly called 'the catastrophic Iraq War'[110] has also produced a painful dilemma in the sense that continued military engagement will risk further alienation, while military disengagement might suggest to the enemies of the USA that violence against it was, in fact, effective. Hugely costly in terms of life and economic damage, the 2003 invasion of Iraq has destabilized much of the region; and the USA has been unable to pacify the country in the face of much opposition to the occupation.[111]

Richard Clarke has commented bleakly of the post-9/11 era that 'Many thought that the Bush administration was doing a good job of fighting terrorism when, actually, the administration had squandered the opportunity to eliminate al-Qaeda and instead strengthened our enemies by going off on a completely unnecessary tangent, the invasion of Iraq.' This adventure was, in Clarke's telling words, 'an unnecessary and costly war in Iraq that strengthened the fundamentalist, radical Islamic terrorist movement worldwide ... Nothing America could have done would have provided al-Qaeda and its new generation of cloned groups a better recruitment device than our unprovoked invasion of an oil-rich Arab country.... Nowhere

on the list of things that should have been done after September
11 is invading Iraq.'[112] And amnesia has played a part here in the
broader failings of the War on Terror. Commenting on the United
States's post-9/11 policy regarding terrorism, leading terrorism
expert Louise Richardson has observed that 'Human lives have
been lost because of the US government's failure to understand the
nature of the enemy we face and its unwillingness to learn from the
experiences of others in countering terrorism.'[113]

There are those who have claimed that, by mid-2007, al-Qaeda
was in fact stronger than ever: 'Al-Qaeda is a more dangerous enemy
today than it has ever been before.... thanks largely to Washington's eagerness to go into Iraq rather than concentrate on hunting
down al-Qaeda's leaders, the organization now has a solid base of
operations in the badlands of Pakistan and an effective franchise in
western Iraq.'[114] This possibly overstates the case, but it is true that
the situation within Iraq has been near-catastrophic in places, and
that this has had malign international effects in terms of sustaining
terrorism. One very prominent politician who was deeply involved
in the government of post-2003 Iraq (Ali A. Allawi) has candidly
observed the extent of the problem, noting 'the chaotic nature of
the country and the terrible passions that had been unwittingly, or
otherwise, unleashed by the invasion and occupation', and lament-
ing angrily 'the way that the country was being grotesquely mismanaged and misdirected'.[115]

General Sir Mike Jackson, head of the British Army during the
2003 invasion, has himself been very critical of his US allies for the
way in which they dealt with the post-war administration of Iraq,
and has criticized the US-led War on Terror as flawed because of
its over-reliance on military power rather than on diplomacy and
nation building.[116] Certainly, not enough thought had been given
in Washington to the problem of post-war reconstruction and to
planning for what would happen after the hostilities were over.[117]

Our definition of terrorism noted the overlap between the
various kinds of violence often involved, and the anti-American
insurgents in Iraq—those violently opposed to the US presence—
exemplify this with their mixture of insurgent and terrorist acts.

The prominence here of suicide bombings encapsulates the central point at issue: namely, that our understanding of what sustains terror must involve key recognition of the frequent role of foreign military occupation as one factor. As Robert Pape has suggested:

> [T]he West's strategy for this war [on terrorism] is fundamentally flawed. Right now, our strategy for the war on terrorism presumes that suicide terrorism is mainly a product of an evil ideology called Islamic fundamentalism and that this ideology would produce campaigns of suicide terrorism wherever it exists and regardless of our military policies. This presumption is wrong and is leading toward foreign policies that are making our situation worse. Although multiple factors are at work, consideration of the most prominent suicide attacks in 2005 shows that the strategic logic of suicide terrorism—and especially the presence of Western combat forces in Iraq and on the Arabian Peninsula—remains the core factor driving the threat we face.[118]

With Iraq having helped further stimulate anti-Western jihadism, the threat of terrorist attacks remains strong. This is true not only of the USA, but of its closest ally, the United Kingdom, too,[119] as is publicly acknowledged by the authorities there. Moreover, this high threat involves people who are, as the head of MI5 Eliza Manningham-Buller admitted in 2006, partly motivated by 'their interpretation as anti-Muslim of UK foreign policy, in particular the UK's involvement in Iraq and Afghanistan'.[120]

It is not that the Afghan and Iraqi missions have had uniformly disastrous results. As noted, real damage was done to al-Qaeda with the uprooting of their Taliban-supported base, and the removal of Saddam Hussein's appalling regime was, in itself, surely highly desirable. And jihadist terrorism was not itself created by these policies: it is true that the London bombings of 2005 and the Madrid bombings of 2004 occurred in a post-Iraq context; but the Bali bombings of 2002 preceded it. Still, there can be little doubt that the Afghan War and (especially) the Iraq War exemplify the central reality, that counter-terrorist military occupation and friction can act as one of the major factors sustaining serious terrorist threats[121] (and this, of course, is a point historically echoed by other powerful historical cases, such as the rise of Hezbollah in Lebanon).

Other aspects of our argument regarding the sustenance of terrorism can also be seen in non-Irish historical settings. The role of sincere commitment, of a profound desire for political change allied to a belief in the strategic necessity of violence to obtain it, of an ideologically powerful tradition and legitimating argument, of the interaction of various key aspects of people's experience (political, religious, economic, cultural) all pointing in the same direction, of inspiring leaders and of the role of organizational dynamics themselves, of the emotional pull of revenge, of the teaching and transmission of political argument and propaganda—these elements can be repeatedly detected throughout the long history of terrorism, from Spain to Israel/Palestine to Lebanon to Chechnya to Italy to Germany and beyond.

Another factor in the sustenance of IRA violence was the support of external actors (whether US sympathizers or Libyan allies), and again this has been a major feature of other historical cases. Not only has there been a stressing of the internationalization of one's cause, as with those involved in anti-colonial struggles in Cyprus (by EOKA) and in Algeria (by the FLN). More directly, the role of state sponsorship has been important in sustaining some serious terrorist campaigns. As the leading expert on state sponsorship, Dan Byman, has pointed out, 'During the 1970s and 1980s, almost every important terrorist group had some ties to at least one supportive government'; 'many terrorist groups regularly receive state support'.[122] As another expert commentator has suggested, terrorism at times became 'an institutionalized form of foreign policy for many nations'.[123]

States have sponsored terrorism for various reasons—strategic, ideological, domestic-political—and in doing so they have at times transformed the nature of the group being sponsored. State support enhances a terrorist group's capacity, although it can also restrain its activities by limiting the range of actions to those favouring the sponsor's own aims. Active sponsorship has involved the decision of a state to assist, fund, arm, train, protect, or give sanctuary to terrorists (and this of course includes cases where the USA itself has backed groups such as Nicaraguan Contras, the Afghan mujahidin, and others). State sponsorship of terrorism has diminished since the end of the Cold War, with the Soviet Union and its allied states being out of the picture. But the important roles of Pakistan in aiding the 1990s Taliban, and of the Afghan Taliban themselves in providing the basis for terrorist development, constitute important exceptions. For even an emphatically non- or trans-state group like al-Qaeda has benefited vitally from state backing (such as that from Afghanistan and Sudan).

The importance of state sponsorship can be very clearly seen if one considers the relationship of Hezbollah to Iran. The former has in many ways been a client terrorist group of the latter, with Iran acting as ideological mentor and financial backer, and playing a large part in making Hezbollah important in the 1980s. The Iranian regime was keen to spread the Islamic revolution, and the creation of Hezbollah offered one way of doing this. During the 1980s Hezbollah stayed close to the Iranian political line, and even yet Iranian funding is important to this fellow anti-Israeli group in Lebanon.

State backing can also be less active, with regimes turning a blind eye to activities within their own territory. This can be of huge significance in the sustaining of terrorism, especially with the decline in active sponsorship in recent times. 'Open and active state sponsorship of terrorism is blessedly rare,' but states can foster terrorism also by not acting: not policing borders, not preventing fund-raising, tolerating rather than stopping recruitment. All of this can help terrorists survive and operate, and 'The list of countries that tolerate at least some terrorist activity is long.'[124]

Given all this, *why does terrorism end?* For one feature of the history of terrorism that we need very clearly to recognize is just how many terrorist campaigns and groups do fizzle out.[125] During the 1970s in Western Europe there was a marked prevalence of left-wing terrorism, famously associated with groups such as the German Red Army Faction (RAF) and the Italian Red Brigades. The RAF (also known as the Baader–Meinhof Gang, after leaders Andreas Baader and Ulrike Meinhof) was a self-styled army of the oppressed. Well-educated and largely middle-class by background, the group had leaders who were disenchanted with the society in which their own opportunities were apparently good. (Baader had dropped out of school, Meinhof was a journalist, and another leader—Gudrun Ensslin—was a trainee teacher.) Emerging into action in 1970, the group represented an ultra-leftist revolutionism, according to which the German state was seen as despicably subservient to US capitalist imperialism (with Vietnam and the Middle East representing particular causes of anger). Ostensibly keen to destroy capitalism through violent methods, the RAF is thought to have committed thirty-four murders between 1970 and 1991.

The RAF remains a sharp-edged issue in German memory even several decades later and long after any momentum has departed from the group. As late as May 2007 the German President, Horst Köhler, refused clemency and early release from prison to RAF member Christian Klar (then serving six life sentences for nine murders carried out in the 1970s): there was some strong pressure on Köhler not to allow Klar's release, demonstrating that the episode was still a painful one even after the RAF itself was effectively dead.[126] For the group had formally disbanded in 1998, and its bloody campaign of bombings, shootings, and arson had never gathered around it serious numbers of supporters or sympathizers. The effective international death of hard-leftist ideology clearly played a part in killing off such movements, as did counter-terrorist action in practice, and the lack of any resonance between the group's ideas and popular thinking in Germany; there was no equivalent here of the kind of relationship enjoyed, for example, between successful nationalist groups and their broader national population.

During the same era Italy too experienced significant leftist terrorism. The Brigate Rosse, or Red Brigades, emerged out of 1960s radicalism, the public objective of the group being 'to mobilize, to extend, and to deepen the armed initiative against the political, economic, and military centres of the imperialist state of the multinationals'.[127] During the 1970s Italy experienced considerable violence (not just from the left, it should be said), but the Brigate Rosse had effectively declined as a serious force by the 1980s. Again a mixture of international ideological and political climate, counter-terrorist success, and a lack of popular resonance, between them, managed to kill off the project. There are, therefore, some echoes of our earlier-established pattern: in the case of this leftist Euroterrorism of the 1970s and 1980s we again see the inefficacy of terrorist violence to achieve its main goals; the role of international political and ideological dynamics in the decline of terrorism; the impact of economic and political realities (not many serious observers by 1990 thought that communism rather than capitalism offered the most viable economic route forward through history); the important role of legitimacy (with the vast majority of Italian and German people satisfied with the existing order, and with few therefore sharing a sense of being at war with capitalism or with either of the two states concerned); and the absence of those kinds of psychological-revanchist, religiously powerful, or culturally supportive aspects of the terrorists' cause which would be needed in order to make it endure.

In explaining why terrorism ends, we need, therefore, both to acknowledge the multi-causal roots of the process in any given setting and also to disaggregate explanations into their different settings while recognizing what family resemblances there are between cases. It is true, for example, that certain processes of counter-terrorist policy (breaking people under interrogation, offering inducements to terrorists to cooperate with the state, using those who have lost their previous faith) can be found across many settings; but it is also important to recognize that this is far less likely in itself to break a resonant nationalist movement than it is to defeat much smaller and cult-like terrorist groups. Moreover, even where there are noisy echoes between groups' experiences—as with the Basque and Irish cases, perhaps—disaggregation and distinction are also important. Many of the features of twenty-first-century ETA's condition might be thought to echo those of the IRA (including the increased difficulty of operating in a post-9/11 climate, or the eroding effect of the broader community's preference for non-violent methods). Yet the two groups' peace process trajectories have not matched one another. A 1998 ETA ceasefire came to an end in 1999, and beyond this an ETA explosion in early January 2007 at Madrid airport (which killed two people, and brought to an end a nine-month ETA truce) showed that there could be very different routes even for apparently similar kinds of group.

In learning from Irish history, we attempted to assess the degree to which terrorism works, and the broader international version of this question is one of the most important for us all to address. (For one thing, serious assessment of its effectiveness will be a necessary basis for any consideration of the justification for, and the supposed morality of, terrorist behaviour.) There are those among the scholarly community who argue that terrorism is indeed an effective way of coercing governments into making policy concessions: 'Terrorism often works. Extremist organizations such as al-Qaeda, Hamas, and the Tamil Tigers engage in terrorism because it frequently delivers the desired response.'[128] Or again, 'The real root cause of terrorism is that it is successful—terrorists have consistently benefited from their terrorist acts.... Terrorism will persist because it often works, and success breeds repetition.'[129] Yet again, in the words of another expert, 'Contemporary terrorism has a very high capacity for achieving its broadest and most typical first strategic objective, the wrecking of normalcy and political order.'[130]

It's certainly true that terrorist violence propels the relevant issue at stake from frequent obscurity towards the front of the world's mind; that it can discredit or delegitimize a government or regime; that it can cause extensive economic disruption and damage; and that it can be effective in achieving short-term results of note, including the release of prisoners or the concession of other specific and immediate demands. The efficacy of terrorist violence can also be seen (as we have noted) when it prompts states to act in ways which backfire against those states and which therefore yield greater support for the terrorists' cause. So the history of terrorist violence does include many instances which lend weight to the arguments of the scholars quoted above. On 23 October 1983, for example, a Hezbollah suicide bomb attack on Beirut US Marine barracks killed 241 US marines, sailors, and soldiers (together with five civilians). The US forces were there as part of a multinational force which had been sent to Beirut in order to bring stability, following the June 1982 Israeli invasion of Lebanon. But the October 1983 attack helped convince the United States to withdraw its forces from Lebanon, and by early 1984 the Marines had duly departed. (Osama bin Laden has been among those who have pointed to this episode as a supposed demonstration that America is too pusillanimous to endure a fight and that terrorist violence can work against it.)

Again, in May 2000 Israel unilaterally withdrew its occupying forces from southern Lebanon under pressure from Lebanese (terrorist/guerrilla) fighters who included Hezbollah. And the latter's apparently successful role in standing up militarily to Israel has had an effect beyond Hezbollah itself. The Hezbollah stance against Israel has helped to inspire Palestinians living under Israeli occupation to pursue their own violence against Israel. Further back in history, one could make a case that the violence of the 1944–8 Jewish revolt, or of EOKA in the 1950s, illustrated the efficacy of terrorism[131] (and that such violence has perhaps had greatest effect when associated with national movements in struggles reflecting the overlap between terrorist and guerrilla violence).

But there are other terrorism experts who take a very different view on the question of whether history teaches that terrorism actually works: 'terrorism has achieved little of any consequence. No government has fallen because of its attacks, comparatively few casualties have been sustained, and no terrorist group has achieved anything more than a fraction of its long-term aims';[132] terrorism 'has been remarkably unsuccessful in gaining strategic objectives': 'As a weapon against well-established liberal democracies or against indigenous autocracies, terrorism has proved an almost total failure.'[133] Such views now abound among terrorism scholars (one of whom carried out a study of the twenty-eight groups listed by the US State Department as foreign terrorist organizations after 2001, discovering that 'terrorist groups rarely achieve their policy objectives'; that 'terrorist success rates are actually extremely low'; and that terrorism is 'a decidedly unprofitable coercive instrument'[134]).

Absolutely crucial here is the fact that, historically, terrorists have rarely achieved their central goals.[135] In the case of Palestinian violence, for example, it has been forcefully argued that terrorism has produced significant rewards and results, and indeed that 'Palestinian terrorism is the paradigmatic example of terrorism that has worked.'[136] But Palestinian terrorism has emphatically *not* achieved the ostensibly central goals of most of those who have practised it, and at the time of writing, it seems no nearer to doing so. Other cases might lend weight to similar assessments: anarchist terrorism, for example, was spectacularly unsuccessful in producing the kind of effect that was desired by its practitioners.[137]

Some of the dynamics here and elsewhere are familiar already from our Irish case. Far from terrorist violence possessing an incrementally, cumulatively greater and more irresistible power over the years, the opposite appears to be nearer to the truth. The longer a particular campaign of terrorism continues, the less striking the public impact and shock, and the more habitual the enemy's capacity to endure such attacks. Even in the case of spectacularly famous violence, it has been again and again clear that central objectives have not been achieved. To take two different and distant cases, we might consider Munich in 1972 and Oklahoma in 1995. In September 1972 terrorists from Black September (a Palestinian group founded in 1971) utilized the huge media possibilities of the Munich Olympic Games—which were being attended by around 6,000 journalists—when they took over a dormitory in the Olympic Village, killing two and seizing as hostages nine more Israeli athletes. The latter were eventually killed also, as the crisis reached its bloody end at an airport where the West Germans launched an attack in which five of the terrorists and one policeman also died.[138] Twenty-three years later, on 19 April 1995, the Alfred P. Murrah Federal building in Oklahoma City was destroyed by a huge truck bomb which killed 168 people and left hundreds more injured.[139] These attacks were both globally and lastingly famous in spectacularly unusual manner. But the political goals of neither the anti-government, idiosyncratic patriot Timothy McVeigh (one of the Oklahoma bombers) nor the violent Palestinian liberation movement Fatah (of which Black September was an offshoot) have come even close to fulfilment.

Moreover, while it is clear that terrorism has, historically, changed the world on many occasions, much of that change has taken forms unanticipated (and not sought) by the agents of violence. As one leading authority has put it, 'Sometimes terrorist actions lead to major consequences that are different from what the terrorists anticipated.'[140] This gap between intentions and outcomes is clear even in a case such as 9/11, which might be judged in part to have served jihadist aims by prompting the USA into counter-productive military response. For the effect of that response has been to intensify anti-US anger and sustain jihadist violence, but not to bring about the central goals which lie behind, for example, Osama bin Laden's politics. Since 9/11, and in direct opposition to bin Laden's own preferences, the United States has in fact greatly *increased* troop levels in the Persian Gulf, attempted to *strengthen* its relations with pro-Western leaders in Muslim countries such as Pakistan and Saudi Arabia, engaged in counter-terrorist policies which have led to the deaths of thousands of Muslims, and strongly continued to support Israel. It is not that 9/11 had no effect, or even that it had no positive effect according to the thinking of those who supported it. It is rather that the central aims which lay behind it have in many cases been rendered even further from practical achievement.

And while it is true that terrorists can provoke states to engage in some counter-productive policies, it is also true that terrorists' own violence can backfire against the cause for which it is carried out. Even in cases where there exists some strong minority basis of support for violence among the wider community, attacks on civilians in particular can have a negative impact in terms of popular sympathy for the struggle. This has repeatedly been evident in Basque Spain and also in Northern Ireland, for example.

Any serious assessment of whether terrorism has worked throughout history will of necessity, in the end, reach an ambiguous conclusion. The complexity and variation of the phenomenon have been too great for a simple or neat answer to be offered. For terrorist groups to endure for long periods might itself be seen as a triumph of resistance, as could be claimed for groups as varied as Hamas, ETA, the UVF, or the IRA. And even those experts who have stressed terrorism's overall failure can recognize that it has had some successes: 'although it is clear that terrorism rarely, if ever, wins strategic political goals, it has an impressive record in gaining such things as massive world-wide publicity, extortion of large ransom payments, and the release of considerable numbers of imprisoned terrorists'.[141]

But even though terrorism can spectacularly highlight the significance of a political root problem, the historical record does point clearly towards some profound limits to its effectiveness. The problem made more urgent of redress is often also made more difficult to solve, precisely because of the polarization, blood investment, and lack of trust which have been engendered by the violence itself. The primary, central aims of terrorist groups have not tended to be achieved, and have frequently been impossibilistic in nature anyway. The clichéd notion of terrorists subsequently becoming vindicated statespersons is probably deceptive too, for the historical record demonstrates numerous ambiguities here. The fact that a former terrorist later becomes a politician does not in itself prove that they were the best of all possible statespersons to have emerged, that their earlier actions were necessary to achieve progress or were justified, or even that their role as perpetrators of terrorizing violence has come to an end. The list of names often deployed in the terrorist-to-statesperson argument includes Nelson Mandela, Jomo Kenyatta, George Washington, Gerry Adams, and Robert Mugabe—a list which clearly demonstrates the ambiguity of the process.

Even those cases in which some serious success has been achieved can, on close inspection, reveal a more messy story. Quite rightly, people point to the effectiveness at times of Hezbollah violence. But even here there are blurred aspects of the story, as is shown by the 2006 Hezbollah war against Israel (prompted by the Hezbollah capture of Israeli soldiers on 12 July in that year). In Lebanon this conflict left a huge reconstruction bill, caused massive economic damage, destroyed tourism for a time, and left more than 1,000 dead civilians. In referring to this 2006 war, Hezbollah leader Hassan Nasrallah said in an interview on Lebanese television on 27 August 2006 that 'If any of us [on the fifteen-member political military council of Hezbollah] had a one per cent concern that Israel was going to reply in this savage manner we would not have captured those soldiers.'[142]

Two final points need to be made at this stage. First, there is the difficulty of disentangling the effect of terrorist violence from that of other factors. Just as a group might claim that its violence was essential to some political initiative, so also a counterfactual opposing argument can be offered in those cases where violence seems to have had an effect: can we know that equal or preferable change might not have been achieved in the absence of terrorism? The fact that terrorist effect seems greatest where the violence is least isolated from other forms of campaigning does not resolve this question either way, but it does point to its profound significance as we evaluate the efficacy or otherwise of this bloody tactic.

Second, there is the question of proportionality. One certainty of terrorist campaigns is that they will cause horrific personal destruction and pain; given the historical lesson that such violence produces many unanticipated effects, one needs centrally to ask whether certain destruction is a morally justifiable cost to pay for a very uncertain outcome. Indeed, there are those who claim that exponents of *non*-violence not only have all the best moral tunes, but might also be the ones with the more effective method in any case: 'while there is often a moral argument for non-violence, the core of the belief is political: that non-violence is more effective than violence, that violence does not work'.[143]

4

HOW SHOULD WE RESPOND?

The first three chapters of this book each began with a summer episode: IRA Army Council members playing peacefully with the UK Prime Minister's children in 1999; a brutal 1975 ETA killing in the Basque country; the IRA's armed campaign officially coming to an end in the same month in 2005 as the 7/7 bombers struck London. But let's now briefly accelerate forward through history to a hypothetical future summer, during which jihadists might successfully strike an American target. Let's imagine a hideous but conceivable event of such proportions—say an Improvised Nuclear Device attack, causing large-scale fatalities—as to jolt the United States with a blow comparable in shocking effect to 9/11. In the wake of such an atrocity the US government would, of course, feel the need to respond in appropriately grand manner. In all likelihood, many of the same kinds of response as followed 9/11 would again ensue: military engagement abroad, legislative changes at home, capture and incarceration and interrogation of suspected terrorist enemies, and so on.

Scholars would be exaggerating the importance of their research and arguments if they thought that, in such a crisis, governments would act as scholars might prefer or advise. But I do think that it's perfectly reasonable to suggest, first, that effective public policy in relation to terrorism might be more achievable if policy-makers reflected on a careful analysis of relevant historical experience; second, that scholars have a serious role to play in providing such careful analysis; and third, that scholars in this field have a duty to put together a coherent and practical argument concerning what would, in fact, be the best response to terrorism, whether in crisis moments or between them.

At the beginning of this book, indeed, I argued that we face two kinds of terrorist problem: the analytical and the practical. Having tried to deal with the former (in terms of interlinked arguments concerning definition, explanation, and history), I want now to address the more practical problem of response, and to do so on the basis of the arguments which have been proffered in the previous chapters of the book. This approach involves important attention to long pasts and to dangerous futures. As we've already noted, terrorism is a very old phenomenon, and we should use this to our advantage in learning what we can from this grim aspect of history. But the issue is of greatest importance because of what we are likely to face ahead; and an understanding of how best to respond to terrorism is most urgent at those moments of unanticipated crisis which puncture human history, such as the hypothetical future summer alluded to above.

Our political record here to date is far from inspiring, not least in our response to the most recent of major terrorist challenges. One sage observer has referred to the post-9/11 War on Terror as having been 'disastrously mismanaged',[1] and I fear that there is much accuracy in this judgement. The deepest challenge for the future is to try to avoid the repetition of misunderstanding and misdiagnosis, so that a durably available answer can be offered to the question of how to respond to the terrorist problem.

Given the magnifying impact of terrorism upon world affairs when it is amplified through state response, this practical problem is one of huge proportions. The most serious danger currently posed by terrorists is probably their capacity to provoke ill-judged, extravagant, and counter-productive state responses, rather than their own direct actions themselves (which statistically continue to represent a comparatively limited danger[2]). Indeed, taking into account the scale of American power and of likely US response to further atrocities, it might be argued that the question of responses to terrorism is central today to what followers of Thomas Hobbes would recognize as the key issue in world politics: the attempt to avoid the process by means of which persistent clashes of interest or of perceived goods result in something akin to civil war.

So, given what we have argued regarding definition, explanation, and history, what can we say about the problem of response? There seem to me to be seven key points, and all of them draw upon what has been argued in our previous three chapters.

First, learn to live with it. One of the depressing lessons from the history of terrorism is that it is always likely to be with us. On Monday 7 October 1985 a group of Palestinians seized an Italian cruise liner, the *Achille Lauro*, after it left Alexandria in Egypt with hundreds of people on board. The hijackers called for the release of Palestinian prisoners then being held in Israel and Italy, and they threatened to kill US passengers on the ship if Egyptian radio and television failed to broadcast their demands. Their leader declared that 'The first to pay with their lives will be the American hostages,'[3] and a Jewish American (Leon Klinghoffer) was indeed killed. This brutal act was seemingly rendered more awful both by Klinghoffer's age—he was in his late sixties—and by the fact that he was in a wheelchair. Early in the First Act of John Adams's subsequent opera based on these events, *The Death of Klinghoffer* (completed in 1991 during the First Gulf War), one of the characters reports that 'We've terrorists on board the ship.'[4] Given the durability of the problem which terrorism represents, and its combination of widespread prevalence and persistence, this line might sadly serve as a political reality for all of us: 'We've terrorists on board.'

For terrorism 'has been with us for centuries,'[5] and it is almost certain to outlive anybody reading this book. From early in recorded history there have been acts which could be defined as terroristic, and even in its modern sense the term and its associated phenomena have been with us for too long for us to be able to assume their foreseeable disappearance. Despite its ambiguous effects, such violence is too tempting a form of warfare to be likely to dissolve; it is unlikely to be extirpated; there are many groups—as we have seen again and again historically—which are partly sustained by sincere and long-term terrorist commitment and belief; and so we are going to have to learn to live with terrorism as part of our political reality.

The literary record serves as a nice refraction of this fact. Reference was made earlier to novelists' accounts of terrorism, from Joseph Conrad to John Updike, and many other examples abound. John Buchan's *The Power-House* (written and set in 1913, but published as a book in 1916[6]) tells of an international, clandestine, anarchist conspiracy at war with civilization. (And, incidentally, Buchan's 1916 novel *Greenmantle* demonstrates that European anxiety regarding the danger posed by Islamic jihad is likewise nothing new: 'Islam is a fighting creed, and the mullah still stands in the pulpit with the Koran in one hand and a drawn sword in the other.'[7]) Writing in 2003, one observer suggested that 'Almost all the terrors that afflict us at the beginning of the present century, in fact, were anticipated in the cheap fiction of a hundred years ago.'[8] This reflects a particular version of the wider international pattern. From the Fenian attacks of the nineteenth century onwards, the UK—like all major states—has had to face the terrorist threat; and it remains a prominent part of daily life as there arise reasonably frequent panics regarding potential or actual attacks. This was evident, for a recent example, in the attempted car bombings in London and Glasgow in the summer of 2007:[9] security crackdowns resulted, along with a public sense that, in the words of one prominent newspaper's editorial, 'The terrorist threat is as real as ever.'[10] And other serious UK papers had earlier carried a similar message ('official warnings about a serious terror threat are based on fact, not hysteria', as a *Guardian* editorial put it in May 2007[11]).

Indeed, the United Kingdom's lengthy experience of terrorism usefully exemplifies the way in which different waves of experience follow one another. Certain battles might fizzle out, just as the Provisional IRA story might finally now have come to an end in the early twenty-first century. But close inspection of the Irish story suggests, in fact, the very durability of this type of problem rather than its ephemeral quality. There was the long Irish republican pre-history of the modern IRA, a republican tradition of paramilitary aggression which stretched back long before the foundation of the Provisionals themselves in 1969, and indeed well back into the nineteenth century. Before this late twentieth-century Provisional

IRA, there had been others bearing the same name and carrying on violence in pursuit of Irish freedom. The Irish revolution of 1916–23, the IRA's bombing campaign in Britain during 1939–40, the same organization's Border Campaign in Ireland of 1956–62—all of these demonstrate the degree to which Irish republican political violence has been a long-term rather than merely recent phenomenon. Moreover, even with the apparent end of the Northern Ireland Troubles in the early twenty-first century, there remains a potential threat within Northern Ireland of lower-level paramilitary violence from other groups (whether Irish republican or Ulster loyalist). And even if all Northern Irish paramilitarism were now completely ended, the United Kingdom's current experience in any case points to the persistence of terrorism rather than to its evaporation. For another set of adversaries (Islamist this time, rather than Irish) has already picked up the bomb and begun to run with it. Terrorism itself is not going to evaporate, even though specific terrorist groups and threats will eventually do so. Particular terrorist campaigns end; terrorism does not.

In this sense, the concept of the War on Terror has to be viewed as only partly appropriate. As our definition of terrorism suggested, there's nothing inherently peculiar about seeing counter-terrorism as involving a species of warfare, since that is really what terrorism itself arguably involves. But the War on Terror as outlined in the manner already quoted from President Bush—'Our War on Terror begins with al-Qaeda, but it does not end there. It will not end until every terrorist group of global reach has been found, stopped and defeated'[12]—might seem less well conceived. Wars end; this one, as set out here, cannot do so. The overall war against terrorism as such is not winnable: we cannot utterly eliminate terrorism, and to talk as if we can is unhelpful.[13] Louise Richardson has aptly responded to this aspect of post-9/11 US policy and its failings:

> [W]e cannot defeat terrorism by smashing every terrorist movement. An effort to do so will only generate more terrorists, as has happened repeatedly in the past. A policy informed by the work of the terrorism studies community would never have declared a global war on terrorism, because we know that such a war can never be won....A policy

informed by those of us who have studied this subject for years would never have had as an objective the completely unattainable goal of obliterating terrorism and would have sought, instead, the more modest and attainable goal of containing terrorist recruitment and constraining resort to the tactic of terrorism.[14]

Such stress on containment fits better with the learn-to-live-with-it response, and can be pursued in the more comforting knowledge that the history of terrorism points often enough towards the durability rather than the destruction of states which are under terrorist attack. This was certainly true of the Northern Ireland experience, despite the impressive longevity, ingenuity, and commitment of the Provisional IRA. And I think that there is a similar, broader lesson to be learned from other historical cases too: 'liberal democracies have been extraordinarily resilient in withstanding terrorist attempts to coerce them into major changes of policy or surrender in the face of the terrorists' demands'.[15] We may require extraordinary patience in dealing with terrorism,[16] but we can do so with some confidence that states will endure resiliently.

While terrorism as such will always be with us, particular terrorist campaigns will usually come to an end. As noted, any proper explanation of terrorism tends towards disaggregation into various settings, and this leads to the second broad point to be learned about practical response: *where possible, address underlying root problems and causes.* We observed that, appalling though it is, terrorist violence is not only inextricably political,[17] but often emerges out of very serious problems regarding matters such as contested state legitimacy and ethnic or national disaffection. Much of what we see as terrorism is generated by such root problems. This in no way necessarily legitimizes such violence, but it does explain it and point towards the vital lesson that ultimately the best way of removing the terrorist symptom is to address the political source, where this is feasible. It is not that political injustice has of necessity driven the terrorist towards violence, but rather that the resolution of underlying problems might indeed lessen or even—in some cases—remove the likelihood of that violence continuing in sustained manner.

This will not always be possible. Those settings, for example, in which self-determination is presented as an answer to a conflict very often turn out to be contexts within which it is very difficult to find agreement about the proper 'self' to do the 'determining'. Contested legitimacy and self-determination have been central to the violence in Israel/Palestine, Spain, Chechnya, Ireland, Kashmir, and Sri Lanka, and even this short list demonstrates both the difficulty and the variability involved in trying to resolve the generative conflict underlying awful violence. We have to be realistic in recognizing what can, and what can not, reasonably be expected to be done; and it will not always be possible for terrorism to be replaced by more conventional politics. (I rather like Michael Burleigh's acidic remark here that 'If you imagine that Osama bin Laden is going to evolve into Nelson Mandela, you need a psychiatrist rather than an historian.'[18]) This reinforces the importance of full *explanation* of what is going on in each unique setting; and arriving at such understanding of what we are actually dealing with in each case is only obtainable if we look very closely at particular *histories*.

But there can be no adequate response to terrorism which ignores those possibilities which do exist to address root problems and, at the very least, to avoid aggravating or accentuating them. Disputed state or regime legitimacy raises the likelihood that terrorism will be significant and durable (as with ETA, Hamas, or the IRA)—as opposed to those more trivial and ephemeral groups (the RAF or the Red Brigades) which do not enjoy such fertile settings. In cases where communal anger can be aroused and sustained by perceived denial of legitimate power, in associated denial of recognition for people's communal 'dignity and worth',[19] terrorist campaigns can find reservoirs of support. The fact that al-Qaeda-related sympathy has been generated in relation to the politics of Saudi Arabia, Pakistan, Israel/Palestine, Egypt, Afghanistan, and Iraq forcibly demonstrates this point. Addressing issues of contested legitimacy in these places would not rid the world of terrorism. But it would greatly reduce the extent of support for one particular version of it. A secure, stable, and legitimate Afghanistan might, in itself, make a significant difference to the prevalence of the international terrorist threat. And here our recognition of the interwovenness of politics, religion, culture, and economics is vital: no secure Afghan arrangement will emerge from an approach which ignores any of these elements, or which refuses to acknowledge that violence is produced by their lethal and distinctive mutual interaction.

It has been claimed by some that we offer encouragement to terrorists if we try to attend to root causes. Harvard Professor Alan Dershowitz, for example, has strongly argued that attempting to address the root causes of terrorism indicates that the tactic has greater efficacy: 'We must take precisely the opposite approach to terrorism. We must commit ourselves *never to try to understand or eliminate its alleged root causes*, but rather to place it beyond the pale of dialogue and negotiation.' According to Dershowitz, far too much encouragement was given to terrorists during the late twentieth century: 'the international community responded to terrorism between 1968 and 2001 by consistently rewarding and legitimizing it, rather than punishing and condemning it'.[20] It is certainly true that to demonstrate the efficacy of terrorism is to encourage its future adoption. But I think it is possible to argue that addressing root causes can involve the demonstration of exactly the opposite lesson: that it is only when they eschew prior terrorism and engage in more conventional politics instead that terrorists can reach any resolution of root problems. In the Northern Ireland case, we have seen that the very Peace Process itself was based on the recognition by the IRA (and its loyalist counterparts) that terrorist violence was not having the desired effect. Negotiations about root causes were therefore founded on the failure of terrorism to yield anticipated victory, and part of the Provisional movement's thinking in pursuing politics rather than war was that it would gain more popular support by taking this new path. Again, therefore, the politics of root causes vindicated non-violent rather than violent action. And, in this sense, there is nothing necessarily incompatible between trying to deal with the political problems which underlie terrorism and demonstrating that peaceful politics are more fruitful and attractive and feasible and effective.

It is true that in some cases it is quite impossible to sort out what the terrorists themselves consider to be root problems: jihadists pursuing the destruction of the USA and the establishment of their own version of Islamic world hegemony are pursuing an unrealizable and non-negotiable aim. And compromise is not always possible. It was unsuccessfully pursued in Northern Ireland for decades; more contemporaneously, even where significant Iraqi insurgents express a willingness to open contacts with the occupying forces, to negotiate and possibly to compromise, it seems clear that their terms and those acceptable to the United States have been simply too far apart from one another to be currently workable.[21]

But even in the jihadi case, it's clear that levels of support are contingent upon perceived Western policies involving Israel/Palestine and Iraq, and that careful political initiative could help to restrict the breadth of jihadist support and recruitment. And our argument about definition, explanation, and history clarifies the reasons for at least attempting political resolution where feasible. If terrorism is indeed ineluctably political in nature, then it must be read not in isolated terms but in relation to political legitimacy, economic, social, and political stability, good government, appropriate states, and specific political context. If—as argued earlier in this book—terrorists and their sympathizers are no less rational, practical, and normal than others, then we can use this to advantage by demonstrating (as has happened strikingly in Ireland and, to some extent also, in Basque Spain) that non-violent methods will yield more fruitful results and greater potential for leverage over opponents. If groups have adopted terrorism because they thought it strategically necessary for the achievement of political momentum, then there might be decisive attractions for them in the prospect of a non-violent politics which could in fact yield much greater momentum. If the sustenance of terrorism is partly dependent upon key leadership figures, then the drawing of those figures towards the politics of more peaceful rewards, inducements, and practical engagement in serious politics and negotiation will be vital to the ending of particular terror campaigns. One of the key priorities in responding to the terrorist problem is to persuade the leaders of what are often enough authoritarian and tightly controlled groups that terrorism is less advantageous than other politics. Of necessity, this will involve long-term contact (whether secret or more open) between the authorities and their terrorist opponents; and vital effort must be put internationally into persuading, enticing, or manipulating terrorist leaderships towards a recognition that post-terrorism will prove more fruitful for them than terrorism in their attempt to redress power relations. It is worth here noting the reflections of Tony Blair's chief negotiator in the Northern Irish Peace Process, Jonathan Powell: 'It is very hard for democratic governments to admit to talking to terrorist groups while those groups are still killing innocent people. But on the basis of my experience I think it is always right to talk to your enemy however badly they are behaving. And luckily for this [the Northern Ireland Peace] Process, the British government's backchannel to the Provisional IRA had been in existence whenever required from 1973 onwards.'[22]

Sceptics rightly point out the difficulty in many settings of achieving an end to terror. But this shouldn't dissuade us from pursuing imperfect yet significant resolution to conflict where that is feasible: 'In counterterrorism, it is more important to look at longer-term solutions rather than just short-term violent solutions of the "eye for an eye" type.'[23] In this book I've argued that the emergence and durability of terrorism have historically owed much to resonant and serious issues such as political legitimacy which have underlain the struggle involved; accordingly, attention to these issues—where possible—makes very good sense. And there has been much recent success in working towards the ending of such conflicts, with the post-1990 era witnessing 'a proliferation of peace agreements'.[24]

If our first two responses should be 'learn to live with it' and 'where possible, address underlying root problems and causes', then the third must be: *avoid the over-militarization of response.* While attempting to end those conflicts which can be ended, and while accepting that we will have to live with some form of terrorism, we must try to diminish its level: to contain, thwart, frustrate, reduce, and limit terror in all the ways we can. And a key aspect to this process is the avoidance of over-militarization, the history of terrorism teaching us in particular that large-scale military force used against civilians has tended to be counter-productive. It is not that military aspects should be altogether absent from our response: again, the Northern Ireland case is useful, for here there would have been far worse violence at certain points had the British Army not been able to provide a constraining presence. But a primarily military response to the terrorist problem will almost certainly exacerbate our difficulties, and it has frequently been the case that even very strong formal military power can be lastingly thwarted by terrorist opponents.

Despite the frequent assumption that military retaliation can deter future terrorists, the reality seems very different: 'defeating or diminishing the overall threat of terrorism is not something that either small- or large-scale retaliations have yet been able to achieve'.[25] Indeed, the 2001–7 period has shown again the limitations of militarized response to terrorist crises,[26] with the United States's deployment of heavy military force (in Afghanistan, but especially in Iraq) probably stimulating more than it has stifled terrorist opposition. One recent expert assessment has it that by 2007 the situation in Afghanistan (a major part of the post 9/11 assault on terror) had become extraordinarily problematic. US and NATO forces there were in a profoundly difficult position: 'it is clear that Afghanistan is anything but a stable and secure country. Indeed, the situation in Afghanistan has become extremely volatile'; 'Afghanistan is once again on the edge of a collapse into anarchy and a safe-haven for international terrorism.' US casualties were rising, and the number of terrorist/insurgent attacks was increasing greatly. And serious mistakes had been made, with a failure to appreciate the true identity and nature of the Taliban and the ethnic basis of the insurgency; with a military force largely insensitive to local customs and perceptions; with the failure to establish a legitimate regime (US allies, the Northern Alliance, had no significant Pashtun involvement, and so the Pashtun population of Afghanistan—more than 40 per cent of the people—saw the Alliance as basically alien); and with the heavy-handed tactics of the military on the ground causing great problems, especially in Pashtun areas of the country.

Here, as so often, collateral damage has done great harm, with the killing of innocents and the battering of suspected opponents by US forces generating a vengeful and lasting backlash.[27]

Broadly, the dangers of massive military response have been made clear again and again in history: euphemistically termed collateral damage can erode sympathy among decisive populations, and it tends to validate what terrorist enemies have said critically about you. It can make necessary compromise more difficult to attain, while legitimizing that very terrorism which it was intended to uproot. And this lesson draws on our earlier recognition of what it has been, throughout history, that has sustained terrorist violence: if one key element in this process is the escalation born of tit-for-tat violence, then it makes great sense for the state not to contribute to that process through an over-militarization of response.

Certainly, the more brutal aspects of military response have tended to prove rather ill-suited to counter-terrorist challenges and situations: 'There is a widespread misconception that using terror to defeat terror will ultimately work. On the contrary, the evidence is that this policy is counterproductive';[28] 'Heavy-handed deployment of police or soldiers against entire civilian populations has invariably been one of the best recruiting mechanisms for terrorist organizations. No one appreciates armed men kicking the door down, manhandling women and rifling through possessions, let alone blowing up one's home.'[29]

As already noted, terrorists have recognized the great value to their cause of provoking states into such counter-productive militarization, with the spectacular backfiring of such policies often having a long-term effect. It might be suggested that, as a general rule, counter-terrorist response is ideally much more of a police than a military matter;[30] it might also be concluded that, in particular, anything perceived by potentially hostile populations as foreign military occupation is likely to stimulate rather than undermine terror, especially if there is significant killing of civilians by military forces.

Despite the frequent deployment of soldiers in response to terrorist crises, it is very unlikely that terrorists will be defeated through military means. Eminent soldiers themselves tend to recognize that both they and their terrorist opponents are using military or violent methods as part of a wider, political battle which cannot be won through military mechanisms alone. General Sir Mike Jackson (head of the British Army during the 2003 invasion of Iraq) later observed frankly that:

> Al-Qaeda's end is not terrorism—that is their way of applying the means of violence; its end is the political one of achieving the ascendancy of Islamic fundamentalism. So 'the global war on terrorism' equates to a war on means, which makes little or no sense. Our objective—our end—must be the physical and intellectual defeat of Islamic fundamentalism as a threat to us. To this end, the means certainly include the use of armed force, but also, very importantly, engagement in the battle of ideas. It is here that the US approach [in its post-9/11 War on Terror] is inadequate: it focuses far too much on the single military means. Nation-building and diplomacy are fundamental to demonstrate the advantages of political and economic progress.[31]

Some observers have argued that terrorism is the greatest of contemporary threats: in Alan Dershowitz's words, 'The greatest danger facing the world today comes from religiously inspired terrorist groups—often state sponsored—that are seeking to develop weapons of mass destruction for use against civilian targets.'[32] Whether or not one finds this persuasive, it is also important to note that—historically—the extent and durability of terrorist threats have repeatedly been increased by counter-productive, large-scale military response to smaller initial crises. The over-militarization of crises—from Belfast to Baghdad—has in fact exacerbated the likelihood of major terrorist hostility.

None of this is to suggest that there is a necessary moral equivalence between state action and terrorist atrocity, or between terrorists who deliberately target civilians and a military operation which, though aimed at combatants, produces unintended civilian casualties. Nor is this necessarily criticism of the soldiers involved on the ground, whose bravery and decency are often evident even in counter-productive circumstances.[33] Moreover, it is not the case that military responses have only negative effect: in Afghanistan, some damage was indeed done to al-Qaeda in the early stages of the post-9/11 war; in Iraq, the removal of Saddam Hussein from power was, in itself, surely of profound benefit. The problem is that militarization can simultaneously contain and exacerbate our problem, and it has done so again and again (not least in the Global War on Terrorism since 2001). Over-militarization of response occurred in early-1970s Northern Ireland (the British Army being, in one ex-IRA man's words, the IRA's 'best recruiting agents'[34]), where it helped to set off a cycle of futile violence from which we are only now escaping, decades later. Regrettably, the same pattern has clearly been echoed in Iraq in more recent years.[35]

Where military involvement is most valuable, it tends not merely to reflect high-quality training and professionalism, but also the acquisition and use of detailed, local, accurate intelligence. This leads us to our fourth important lesson in terms of how to respond to the terrorist problem: *intelligence is the most vital element in successful counter-terrorism*. This has been stressed by experts with a variety of backgrounds and views, and it simply cannot be overstated: 'Perhaps 95% of the important action in any campaign against terrorism consists of intelligence and police work: identifying suspects, infiltrating movements, collaborating with police forces in other countries, gathering evidence for trials and so on';[36] 'The secret of winning the battle against terrorism in an open democratic society is winning the intelligence war: this will enable the security forces, using high-quality intelligence, to be proactive, thwarting terrorist conspiracies before they happen.'[37] Sustained human assets— agents and informers who acquire superior intelligence about one's enemy—are vital if one is to possess the necessary understanding of the terrorist opponent. The effective infiltration and penetration of enemy groups, together with the sharp-eyed deployment of electronic and other surveillance, will allow for the gathering of decisive knowledge. Precisely who and where are the terrorists? What is stimulating (and what might undermine) their reservoirs of recruits and sympathizers? What are they currently planning, and when? What are their strengths and weaknesses, their divisions and potential fissures? What is their position in terms of finances and weapons? What are the conditions under which they might consider political compromise?

Investment in the process of acquiring such intelligence is, arguably, the crucial foundation upon which other, interlinked aspects of response can then be built. Without such high-quality intelligence, it is likely that all aspects of state response (legal, military, propagandist) will stumble ineffectively. But, armed with such intelligence, the state can win some tactical victories, and some effective counter-terrorist strategies can be adopted.[38]

History teaches this clearly enough. In Northern Ireland, the state's intelligence operations did not defeat the IRA militarily. But they did greatly limit and constrain its activities, and they contributed towards that stalemate from which the Peace Process was eventually developed.[39] There is some evidence that the United States is now recognizing the primary importance of penetrating radical and terrorist groups;[40] and the USA of course possesses historically unrivalled intelligence and surveillance capacity. But both before and after the 9/11 atrocity, it's clear that there were profound intelligence failures, and that these have significantly contributed to America's terrorist problem. US unpreparedness for 9/11 arose partly from inadequate security coordination. There was also a failure to understand and interpret the mass of data actually in the authorities' possession, and there was a lack of the assets necessary to acquire and informedly monitor essential materials. Pre-9/11, US monitoring of terrorist activity in Afghanistan was woefully inadequate; indeed, around 1996 there was virtually no Western intelligence presence at all in Afghanistan, and so al-Qaeda's reorganization, training, and growth there were able to flourish unmonitored; and, before 11 September, few FBI offices demonstrated sufficient interest at all in the emergent problem of Islamic militancy.[41]

After 2001, the build-up to the Iraq War reflected further serious intelligence failures. US intelligence on Iraqi WMD programmes proved damagingly defective; more broadly, it's now clear that there were American intelligence failures of huge proportions in the run-up to the wars in both Afghanistan and Iraq, and that this problem persisted even during the post-Iraq invasion period.[42] In terms of what was going on in Iraq, in particular, there was a marked failure to gather accurate, precise, up-to-date information.[43] Nor were these difficulties restricted only to the United States. On 6 July 2005 the Director-General of the UK's MI5, Eliza Manningham-Buller, apparently told senior MPs in the House of Commons that there was no imminent terrorist threat to London or to the rest of the country. The following day there occurred the 7 July 2005 suicide bombings.[44]

In short, intelligence-based strategies are absolutely key to the success of counter-terrorism, and this is something increasingly recognized in the terrorism literature.[45] But there is still evidence that the ongoing response to terrorist challenges relies, even yet, too heavily on formal military deployment: on a war-mode response which still lacks the adequate development of accurate, precise counter-terrorist intelligence or planning.[46] Related to this are the claims made by some scholars that—even yet—not enough attention has been paid within the United States, either in decision-making or in journalistic circles, to the vital issue of actually preventing future terrorist attacks.[47]

If intelligence is one vital arena of counter-terrorism conflict, then the legal realm is another, and following the September 2001 attacks on America many countries have introduced new anti-terrorism legislation, greatly expanding the respective authorities' powers for dealing with suspects. Calls for far greater powers of detention remain prominently ongoing: supported by Scotland Yard, one of the UK's most senior police officers (Ken Jones) suggested in the summer of 2007 that the authorities should be given the power to lock up terror suspects indefinitely without charge, as a necessary response to the danger posed by international terror.[48]

But the best response here to the terrorist problem is probably this: *respect orthodox legal frameworks and adhere to the democratically established rule of law*. Staying within the law maintains that important Weberian distinction between legitimate states and their illegitimate terrorist opponents. If states are successfully to maintain a monopoly over the legitimate use of force within their territory, then it is important that they credibly uphold the division between what they do and what their (illegitimate) opponents resort to. To transgress the line which legitimizes you as the state is to risk undermining that on which your own power ultimately rests. Historically, as we have seen, there have been many examples of this problem, including those instances in the UK's dealings with Irish republican opponents which appear to have involved just such transgression. The legacy of shoot-to-kill controversies, for example, has been largely damaging to the UK authorities in Northern Ireland, as has the long-term damage done by boundary-stepping British Army activity in early-1970s Ulster. It is far from clear that transgression of legal boundaries yields sufficient benefit to outweigh the credibility and propaganda costs that are incurred, a point repeatedly seen in relation to the treatment of detainees, for example.[49] In the context of contemporary jihadism, it is worth noting the dramatic contribution made by harsh imprisonment and torture to *stimulating* terrorist violence.[50]

As has been argued, the history of terrorism suggests the durability of states in face of terrorist challenge, and the sustenance of liberal-democratic practice can contribute towards this important effect: 'The government and security forces must conduct all anti-terrorist operations within the law. They should do all in their power to ensure that the normal legal processes are maintained, and that those charged with terrorist offences are brought to trial before the courts of law.'[51] Successful counter-terrorism will rely most heavily on police work, and on respect for the existing legal framework of civilian authority and power. Certainly, normal legal procedures have tended to be less counter-productive and more useful than, say, the incorporation of torture: French experience in torturing Algerian prisoners, for example, produced far less reliable and valuable intelligence than would have been necessary in order to offset the huge damage done in terms of political and public relations; and in the post-9/11 War on Terror, torturing and degrading practices have done little to enhance the effectiveness of the cause.[52]

One aspect of this legal response concerns the issue of civil liberties, the counter-terrorist threat to which is well known and long-standing. Here it is not merely a question of effectiveness—that

the battle against terrorism is more likely to be won by calm professionalism within the existing framework of respecting civil liberties—but also a more central question of what it is that one is
defending in the conflict against terrorist violence in any case. As
this book has argued, terrorism can only properly be explained if
its interwovenness with politics, religion, culture, and economics is
fully recognized. So, too, the response to terrorist challenges is only
properly understood if it is placed in such a wider context. If, as one
leading authority has suggested, civil liberties are best understood
as a necessary part of a broader political story (that civil liberties are
'primarily concerned with the law and practice of political freedom', and that as such they are vital to representative government,
political freedoms, and democratic culture[53]), then it is all the more
important that our struggle against terrorism is in harmony with,
rather than hostile to, these essential aspects of the culture which
we consider to be legitimate. On this understanding, the erosion of
civil liberties is not merely ineffective or even counter-productive:
it is also at odds with our ultimate purpose in countering terror in
the first place: 'The more Western society reacts to terrorist assault
with an answerable illegality, the more it depletes the very spiritual
and political resources which it takes itself to be protecting. . . . In
the drive to safeguard liberty, the West finds itself increasingly in
danger of eradicating it.'[54] 'It is a dangerous illusion to believe one
can "protect" liberal democracy by suspending liberal rights and
forms of government.'[55]

Moreover, the usual mechanisms of the law can indeed contribute very significantly to, at least, the containment or restriction of
terrorism. The long-term imprisonment of large numbers of republican and loyalist prisoners in Northern Ireland was in itself very
important to the process of containment there, and helped to generate the conditions of stalemate out of which the eventual Peace
Process was developed.

Even the most careful deployment of legal process will not, on
its own, defeat terrorism. But the vital thing is to avoid counter-
productive actions, and to learn how to do this through a reading
of historical experience. Rushed legislation amid terrorist crises has

repeatedly been shown to be damaging; and this has been clear again after 2001, when new laws have undermined important civil liberties in moves which have not obviously reduced the likelihood of further attacks on the West.[56] But this was a lesson which could and should have been well learned already.

In Britain during the 1970s, anti-terror legislation was rushed through parliament in the wake of IRA bombs in England: the 1974 Prevention of Terrorism Act, for example, provided for detention without trial and expulsion from Britain.[57] It is far from clear that such initiatives greatly helped in combating the IRA, but they did—unhelpfully for the authorities—seem to make the state appear repressive. And this pattern has been repeated in the early years of the twenty-first century, as again liberal-democratic states have reacted to appalling terrorist violence with measures which seem to validate at least some of their opponents' criticisms.

There are, therefore, both pragmatic and political-philosophical grounds for adhering to the orthodox processes and protections of the law. There are also other features of necessary response which demand urgent commitment, and which have utterly practical dimensions. These might be summarized by the injunction that we should *coordinate security-related, financial, and technological preventative measures*. It is important to be realistic and to recognize that no practical steps towards prevention will be entirely effective. But the history of terrorism does suggest that there are indeed practical ways of limiting terrorist effectiveness, and that these can have life-saving as well as politically significant consequences.

Given the heterogeneous nature of terrorist operations, these ways will involve disruption and thwarting rather than decisive victory; but aspects of this process can still be of value in, for example, the financial realm. Terrorism is, among other things, a very practical business (sometimes literally), and the acquiring, storing, and liberating of funds therefore form major parts of the process. Counter-terrorist financial responses alone will not defeat terrorist activity, but as part of a wider repertoire of responses they can make a contribution. 'Financial and material resources are correctly perceived as the lifeblood of terrorist operations, and governments have determined that fighting the financial infrastructure of terror-ist organizations is the key to their defeat.'[58] Many terrorist opera-tions are under-funded, and, this being the case, terrorists' activity can sometimes be thwarted through the taking of financial steps.

Terrorist funding can, of course, be acquired in various ways, including robberies, kidnappings and hostage-taking, intimidation and extortion, state support, sympathizer donation, credit card fraud, and the establishment and running of legitimate business activities. And there are clear limitations to what can be done in the finan-cial realm of counter-terrorism. For one thing, even some major terrorist operations are reasonably inexpensive: the 2004 Madrid train bombings appear to have cost about $50,000 to carry out, and the 7/7 attacks in London the following year even less; the 1993 attack on the World Trade Center in New York is thought to have cost under $19,000.[59] And even energetic efforts to thwart terror-ists' financial activity can have their limits. Much energy has been expended since 9/11 to prevent the flow of funds to and among terrorist groups; but it is far from clear that post-9/11 financial regu-lations would have ensured that the activities of the perpetrators of 9/11 itself would have been spotted and prevented. Moreover, doubts have been raised about the ongoing effectiveness in recent years of those measures that have been introduced.[60]

Yet there are understandable calls for the interruption of terrorist financial networks to be pursued ('Stopping or at least reducing the flow of money to terrorist organizations can hamper their ability to conduct attacks'[61]); and at times there have been very angry voices raised concerning the tendency of states to tolerate financial (and other) sustaining bases of terrorist activity. Commentator Melanie Phillips's attack on 'Londonistan' serves as a sharp example of the latter. The 7/7 bombings, she claims,

> finally lifted the veil on Britain's dirty secret in the war on terrorism—that for more than a decade, London had been the epicentre of Islamic militancy in Europe. Under the noses of successive British govern-ments, Britain's capital had turned into 'Londonistan'—a mocking play on the names of such state sponsors of terrorism as Afghanistan—and become the major European centre for the promotion, recruitment,

and financing of Islamic terror and extremism.... Incredibly, London had become the hub of the European terror networks.[62]

Part of Phillips's concern lay with the supposed channelling of Islamist funds through banks within Britain. It's doubtful whether enough will be done by the authorities to allay Phillips's own anxiety here. But it is clear that monitoring financial networks can allow both for sometime interception of violent activity and also for the acquisition of valuable intelligence about terrorist operations and organizations.

Intelligence relates also to other aspects of coordinated practical response. If it is true that, as one leading authority has it, 'Order maintenance is probably seen as the elemental task of government',[63] then quotidian practice of security enhancement should indeed be a key state priority. Improving security-preventative measures—at airports and the like—will not rule out terrorism, but history suggests that it will greatly minimize its likely incidence. The hardening of targets (through protective barriers, restricted parking and access, and more expert security checks) forms one part of this; consequence management—preparation for what to do in the event of an attack—forms another.

Post-9/11, steps have, of course, been taken to improve practical and preventative security, the 2003 setting up of the US Department of Homeland Security being one famous example. Perhaps the major priority here should be one alluded to in our discussion of definition: the particularly menacing threat of nuclear terrorism. It is arguable that in 2007 the United States was no safer from nuclear terrorism than it had been in 2001, despite the intervening years of the War on Terror: no truly effective or coherent plan has evolved here, and this requires urgent redress. The dangers are clear enough: 'The huge quantity of fissile material in Russia poses a uniquely dangerous risk of terrorist acquisition of weapons-origin material for an IND [Improvised Nuclear Device]'; currently, we are met with 'the dangers posed by the four faces of nuclear terrorism: the theft and detonation of an intact nuclear weapon, the theft or purchase of fissile material leading to the fabrication and detonation of a crude nuclear weapon, the attack on or sabotage of nuclear installations, and the dispersal of highly radioactive material by conventional explosives or other means.'[64] In response, the implementation of stringent global nuclear security standards is vital, the aim being to secure stocks of nuclear arms and of fissile material, and adequately to protect nuclear facilities. The securing of Pakistan's and Russia's nuclear assets is, perhaps, especially vital.[65]

Coordinated preventative action can and must also adapt to technological fluidity (the utilization of internet technology for counter-terrorist intelligence work being especially valuable, given the degree to which latter-day terrorist groups have used this medium for networking, recruiting, and propaganda). More generally, all practical security measures must be as effectively harmonized and coordinated as possible, in order to avoid the problems frequently generated in the past by failed communication, or even by competition, between allies and between fellow agencies within the counter-terrorist effort.

Turf wars between different wings of the state have historically been a problem in the UK's response to terror (police–MI5 liaison not always proving ideal), and in recent years considerable efforts have rightly been made to achieve a seamlessness of coordination, drawing together the military, intelligence, police, and civil service wings of the operation. Integration and cooperation are vital, too, in inter-state work. Effective response to terrorism will have to be multi- rather than unilateral, and this can involve shared expertise through training, the prompt sharing also of vital intelligence, the utilization (where appropriate) of bodies such as the United Nations, and coordinated efforts to end passive as well as active state sponsorship of terrorist groups.[66] Bilateral agreements between states can make some practical difference, and while there are problems with this long-standing issue of international coordination, 'There is widespread agreement that cooperation and information sharing between law enforcement and intelligence agencies will be vital for prevention of future terrorist attacks, including attempts by terrorists to utilize nuclear weapons.'[67] One problem in the wake of US responses to 9/11 has been the weakening of some international relationships during the War on Terror, and repairing these should be a major priority. Moreover, as we saw earlier, appropriate international intervention and political climate can, on occasion, play a part in leading towards the end of particular terrorist campaigns. Such an effect is made more likely if greater international harmony of response and action can be achieved.

The final link in our chain of appropriate response is to *maintain strong credibility in counter-terrorist public argument*. The history of terrorism demonstrates very clearly the problems which can occur when states undermine their own credibility in their ongoing struggle against terrorist opponents. This has been seen recently in the War on Terror, during which the United States has lost considerable credibility within the Muslim world as a consequence not only of its Iraq policy, but also of the manner of espousing it. To claim that Saddam Hussein had been involved in producing 9/11, and then to have to admit that this was not so; to claim that Saddam possessed WMD, and then admit that none could be found—these have been extraordinarily damaging in their impact on US credibility among those who are the vital constituency to be won over.[68] To promise (and even prematurely claim) victory in Iraq, and then find oneself in an ongoing and long-term war there; to hint at the possibility of victory against terror itself—again, these have been unhelpful.

For credibility is a crucial resource both with your own people and among the pool of potential sympathizers for your terrorist enemies. A comparatively small, but telling, illustration of this can be found in the UK's response to the Provisional IRA. Its presentation of IRA prisoners during the 1970s and early 1980s as merely criminal rebounded against it in the broader nationalist community in Ireland, since even those northern nationalists (the majority) whose nationalism did not lead them to support the IRA knew that the IRA's motivation and character were in fact profoundly political. As a consequence, much damage was done in the relationship between the UK authorities and precisely that population among whom IRA sympathizers could be increased or reduced in number. And the government's subsequent dealings with the IRA demonstrated the dangers of losing trust among your own natural supporters too. One of the enduring difficulties in the Northern

Ireland Peace Process has been the lack of trust in it shown by the majority unionist community in Ulster. Part of this relates to the fact that, for some years, unionists found that they could not trust official pronouncements on the issue, for example, of whether or not British contacts were ongoing with the IRA. The Provisional IRA's most famous opponent, the Revd Ian Paisley, himself told me in 1994 that 'people believe now that the IRA version of their undercover talks with Britain has more truth in it than the [UK] Northern Ireland Office's...something that is very repugnant to me, but it's become a reality, that people have more faith in the statements of the IRA than they have in the statements of the British government'.[69] Part of the reason for the long and painful delay in establishing a lasting deal in Northern Ireland lay in this very problem: that the majority community had lost much faith in the credibility and trustworthiness of its own government.

In the globally much more significant case of post-9/11 US international diplomacy, it is the question of credibility among potential enemies which is of greatest moment. Here, the regime of George W. Bush was lamentably weak, failing to establish either credibility or sufficiently good relations with important possible allies. Walter Russell Mead, an intellectual reasonably sympathetic to elements of the Bush regime's approach, has himself commented that, 'Right or wrong on the substance, the Bush administration has completely failed to make its case to world opinion, and the effect of this ongoing and serious failure has been to provide aid and comfort to our enemies and to complicate virtually all of the tasks of American foreign policy.'[70] In combating terrorism, there is a need to establish good relations with locally influential elites, who can more effectively argue from within the relevant community than outside players can do; a need to avoid spectacularly unpopular policies and interventions; a need to consolidate rather than squander the anti-terrorist sympathy which follows a terrorist atrocity (as, most dramatically, with 9/11), and to recognize and magnify the damage that terrorists' atrocities often do to their own levels of support;[71] a need to stress—in line with the argument of this book—that terrorism is not only appalling in the suffering it causes,[72] but also markedly ineffective in resolving the problems which it makes so world-famous; a need to acknowledge honestly the political and serious basis of the terrorist campaign being faced; a need to build on the essential normality of those people to whom terrorists appeal for support—for instance, in making sure that off-putting atrocities are what the other side does, and that the momentum available through non-violent methods is likely to be greater than that achieved through bombing and killing.

If, as this book has argued, terrorists and their backers are normal and rational, while terrorism itself is a method historically unsuccessful in achieving its central goals, then the war of ideas can be one waged by states with some real confidence. If terrorism emerges because people believe it to be strategically effective in dealing with serious problems of legitimacy and power, then states' clear and credible and patient demonstration of the reverse can have effect. If political realities are closer to states' own analyses than they are to those of their opponents—and our emphasis on honest definition, explanation, and history is vital partly for this reason—then public argument can indeed undermine rather than reinforce terrorist durability. It can legitimately be pointed out, for example, that the Islamist reading of Western culture offered by Sayyid Qutb was deeply (indeed, absurdly) simplistic;[73] and that, in terms of Islamic religious interpretations, there is far greater credibility in many of the Islamic clerics who condemn al-Qaeda than there is in the rather bogus theological standing of people such as Osama bin Laden or Ayman al-Zawahiri (the latter being the torch-bearer for Sayyid Qutb's longed-for campaign and the ideological leader of al-Qaeda). The much-mentioned matter of winning hearts and minds can—at times, and with subtlety—be achieved, even in very difficult circumstances.[74]

But it is essential to be credibly honest in our public arguments here, and not to rely on implausibly simplistic assumptions of straightforward state 'good' versus uncomplicated terrorist 'evil'. Terrorists kill civilians, we announce. Well, say our opponents, what about state bombings? In the words of ex-IRA man Danny Morrison:

If terrorism is the use of indiscriminate or discriminate violence against civilians in order to effect political change or advance a military defeat then certainly the British and US governments have terrorist pasts which they not only refuse to repudiate but uphold as exemplary responses.... Much of the aerial bombing of Germany was aimed at killing civilians and sapping the morale of the German people. In 1945 the US decided to break Japan, rather than lose its own men through invasion, by dropping nuclear bombs on the civilians of Hiroshima and Nagasaki. Israel practises state terrorism by its policy of assassinations and its cavalier attitude to the deaths of Palestinian civilians.[75]

The definition of terrorism outlined in this book, and the approach consequently adopted to explain it, might serve as an antidote to such fruitless arguments between sides merely accusing each other of being the real terrorists.

Terrorism, as leading terrorist expert Martha Crenshaw rightly observed long ago, 'has no easy solution',[76] and the response offered above is certainly not intended as a neat solution to the terrorist problem. But I do think that these interlinked points—integrated as they are with honest arguments about definition, explanation, and history—might provide a more appropriate practical basis for response than has been evident certainly in recent years. Learn to live with it; where possible, address underlying root problems and causes; avoid the over-militarization of response; recognize that intelligence is the most vital element in successful counter-terrorism; respect orthodox legal frameworks and adhere to the democratically established rule of law; coordinate security-related, financial, and technological preventative measures; and maintain strong credibility in counter-terrorist argument—all of these approaches to terrorism have been at least partially or initially ignored in the post-9/11 crisis, on occasion with disastrous consequences. My hope is that this book may make some small contribution towards a debate which will allow us, in future, to respond more persuasively, shrewdly, and effectively to the next stage of our terrorist problem.

ENDNOTES

CHAPTER I

1. J. Powell, *Great Hatred, Little Room: Making Peace in Northern Ireland* (London: Bodley Head, 2008), p. 151.
2. R. English, *Armed Struggle: The History of the IRA* (New York: Oxford University Press, 2005; 1st edn. 2003), pp. 110, 162.
3. E. Moloney, *A Secret History of the IRA* (London: Penguin, 2007; 1st edn. 2002), pp. 378, 380, 526, 583, 688, 697.
4. Patrick Magee, interviewed by the author, quoted in the *Independent on Sunday*, 2 March 2003.
5. C. Gearty, 'Introduction', in C. Gearty (ed.), *Terrorism* (Aldershot: Dartmouth, 1996), p. xi.
6. Quoted in D. J. Whittaker (ed.), *The Terrorism Reader* (London: Routledge, 2003; 1st edn. 2001), p. 3.
7. J. Gearson, 'The Nature of Modern Terrorism', *Political Quarterly*, 73 (Aug. 2002), p. 9.
8. W. Laqueur, *The New Terrorism: Fanaticism and the Arms of Mass Destruction* (London: Phoenix Press, 2001; 1st edn. 1999), p. 5.
9. *Chambers 20th Century Dictionary* (Edinburgh: Chambers, 1983), p. 1335.
10. *The Concise Oxford Dictionary* (London: BCA/Oxford University Press, 1991; 1st edn. 1911), p. 1261.
11. I. Primoratz, 'What is Terrorism?', in Gearty (ed.), *Terrorism*, p. 23.
12. A. H. Kydd and B. F. Walter, 'The Strategies of Terrorism', *International Security*, 31/1 (Summer 2006), p. 52.
13. C. A. J. Coady, 'The Morality of Terrorism', in Gearty (ed.), *Terrorism*, p. 178.
14. C. Gearty, *Terror* (London: Faber & Faber, 1992; 1st edn. 1991), p. 1.
15. R. A. Pape, *Dying to Win: Why Suicide Terrorists Do It* (London: Gibson Square Books, 2006; 1st edn. 2005), p. 9.
16. B. Hoffman, *Inside Terrorism* (London: Victor Gollancz, 1998), pp. 43–4. Another powerful, expansive definition suggests that 'Terrorism is the systematic use of coercive intimidation, usually to service political ends. It is used to create and exploit a climate of fear among a wider target group than the immediate victims of the violence, and to publicize a cause, as well as to coerce a target to acceding to the terrorists' aims.

Terrorism may be used on its own or as part of a wider unconventional war. It can be employed by desperate and weak minorities, by states as a tool of domestic and foreign policy, or by belligerents as an accompaniment in all types and stages of warfare. A common feature is that innocent civilians, sometimes foreigners who know nothing of the terrorists' political quarrel, are killed or injured. Typical methods of modern terrorism are explosive and incendiary bombings, shooting attacks and assassinations, hostage-taking and kidnapping, and hijacking' (P. Wilkinson, *Terrorism Versus Democracy: The Liberal State Response* (London: Frank Cass, 2001; 1st edn. 2000), pp. 12–13).

17. Wilkinson, *Terrorism Versus Democracy*, p. 218. Cf. A. P. Schmid and A. J. Jongman (eds.), *Political Terrorism* (Amsterdam: North Holland Publishing, 1988).

18. M. Juergensmeyer, *Terror in the Mind of God: The Global Rise of Religious Violence* (Berkeley: University of California Press, 2001; 1st edn. 2000), p. 139.

19. Primoratz, 'What is Terrorism?', pp. 18, 22.

20. *Sun*, 8 July 2005.

21. C. von Clausewitz, *On War* (Harmondsworth: Penguin, 1968; 1st edn. 1832), p. 104.

22. Gearson, 'Nature of Modern Terrorism', p. 8.

23. See, for example, the argument that terrorism involves 'the resort to violence for political ends by unauthorized, non-governmental actors in breach of accepted codes of behaviour regarding the expression of dissatisfaction with, dissent from, or opposition to the pursuit of political goals by the legitimate government authorities of the state whom they regard as unresponsive to the needs of certain groups of people' (J. Lodge, 'Introduction' to J. Lodge (ed.), *Terrorism: A Challenge to the State* (Oxford: Martin Robertson, 1981), p. 5. See also the approach adopted in Louise Richardson's excellent book, *What Terrorists Want: Understanding the Terrorist Threat* (London: John Murray, 2006), p. 21.

24. For an impressively calm account of this episode, see A. Guelke, *The Age of Terrorism and the International Political System* (London: I. B. Tauris, 1998; 1st edn. 1995), pp. 194–6.

25. See, e.g., Wilkinson, *Terrorism Versus Democracy*, pp. 19, 41; Juergensmeyer, *Terror in the Mind of God*, p. 5; J. Horgan, *The Psychology of Terrorism* (London: Routledge, 2005), p. 12.

26. D. Della Porta, 'Institutional Responses to Terrorism: The Italian Case', in Gearty (ed.), *Terrorism*.

27. N. Chomsky, *Power and Terror: Post-9/11 Talks and Interviews* (New York: Seven Stories Press, 2003), p. 66.

28. N. Chomsky, *The Culture of Terrorism* (London: Pluto, 1989). Cf. A. George (ed.), *Western State Terrorism* (Cambridge: Polity Press, 1991).

29. M. Burleigh, *Blood and Rage: A Cultural History of Terrorism* (London: Harper Press, 2008), pp. 111–33.

30. The dynamics of states and their actions require extensive definition and analysis within the context of a now vast literature, and it would be unhelpful to treat non-state and state terrorism as though they were essentially the same. For consideration of the state itself, see R. English and C. Townshend (eds.), *The State: Historical and Political Dimensions* (London: Routledge, 1999), and P. Dunleavy and B. O'Leary, *Theories of the State: The Politics of Liberal Democracy* (Basingstoke: Macmillan, 1987).

31. See the thoughtful treatment of this subject offered in R. E. Goodin, *What's Wrong with Terrorism?* (Cambridge: Polity Press, 2006), pp. 50–77.

32. J. Goodwin, 'A Theory of Categorical Terrorism', *Social Forces*, 84/4 (June 2006), p. 2028.

33. D. Byman, 'Friends Like These: Counterinsurgency and the War on Terrorism', *International Security*, 31/2 (Fall 2006), p. 84. Cf. C. C. Combs, *Terrorism in the Twenty-First Century* (London: Pearson Education, 2003; 1st edn. 1997), p. 12; J. Barker, *The No-Nonsense Guide to Terrorism* (London: Verso, n.d.), p. 23.

34. Combs, *Terrorism in the Twenty-First Century*, p. 10.

35. K. Bloomfield, *Stormont in Crisis: A Memoir* (Belfast: Blackstaff Press, 1994), pp. 3, 5.

36. D. K. Gupta, 'Exploring Roots of Terrorism', in T. Bjorgo (ed.), *Root Causes of Terrorism: Myths, Realities and Ways Forward* (London: Routledge, 2005), p. 20.

37. *The Shorter Oxford Dictionary*, i (Oxford: Oxford University Press, 1980; 1st edn. 1933), p. 900.

38. Ibid. p. 1088. A group such as the Colombian National Liberation Army exemplifies this capacity to practise both terrorism and insurgency.

39. Cf. 'terrorism was closely intertwined with insurgencies throughout the twentieth century' (A. K. Cronin, *Ending Terrorism: Lessons for Defeating al-Qaeda* (London: Routledge, 2008), p. 52).

40. Wilkinson, *Terrorism Versus Democracy*, p. 1.

41. M. Levitt, 'Hezbollah Finances: Funding the Party of God', in J. K. Giraldo and H. A. Trinkunas (eds.), *Terrorism Financing and State Responses: A Comparative Perspective* (Stanford, Calif.: Stanford University Press, 2007), p. 136.

42. Nor is this type of phenomenon unique to Lebanon. Hamas (an offshoot of the Palestinian Muslim Brotherhood, created in 1987 during

the Palestinian uprising or intifada against Israeli rule in Gaza and the West Bank) from the start involved terrorist violence; but Hamas has also done far more than just terrorism, its activities involving much broader social and political work as well.

43. L. de Cataldo Neuburger and T. Valentini, *Women and Terrorism* (Basingstoke: Macmillan, 1996; 1st edn. 1992), p. 63.

44. For example, see W. Gutteridge (ed.), *The New Terrorism* (London: Mansell Publishing, 1986), and Laqueur, *New Terrorism*.

45. D. Haubrich, 'Modern Politics in an Age of Global Terrorism: New Challenges for Domestic Public Policy', *Political Studies*, 54/2 (June 2006), p. 419.

46. R. Gunaratna, *Inside Al-Qaeda: Global Network of Terror* (London: Hurst, 2002), p. 1.

47. S. Simon and D. Benjamin, 'America and the New Terrorism', *Survival*, 42/1 (Spring 2000), p. 59.

48. Ibid., p. 66.

49. D. Tucker, 'What is New about the New Terrorism and How Dangerous is It?', *Terrorism and Political Violence*, 13/3 (2001), p. 1; cf. 'much of what passes for "new" terrorism has a long history' (T. R. Mockaitis, *The 'New' Terrorism: Myths and Reality* (Westport, Conn.: Praeger Security International, 2007), p. xii).

50. Tucker, 'What is New about the New Terrorism', p. 9.

51. For valuable analysis of the nuclear terrorist threat, see G. Allison, *Nuclear Terrorism: The Risks and Consequences of the Ultimate Disaster* (London: Constable, 2006; 1st edn. 2004).

52. C. D. Ferguson, W. C. Potter, A. Sands, L. S. Spector, and F. L. Wehling, *The Four Faces of Nuclear Terrorism* (New York: Routledge, 2005), pp. 19, 31, 33, 37, 41, 47, 117; Combs, *Terrorism in the Twenty-First Century*, p. 271; L. Wright, *The Looming Tower: Al-Qaeda's Road to 9/11* (London: Penguin, 2007; 1st edn. 2006), p. 5. It should be noted, however, that al-Qaeda does not exist as it did in its pre-9/11 form; as a more diffuse framework for terrorist activity against the West, however, it still poses some serious threat.

53. Allison, *Nuclear Terrorism*, pp. 15, 120.

54. F. Fukuyama, *After the Neocons: America at the Crossroads* (London: Profile Books, 2006), p. 67. Cf. Ferguson *et al.*, *The Four Faces of Nuclear Terrorism*, pp. 4, 318.

55. R. Elsdon, *Bent World: Science, The Bible and the Environment* (Leicester: Inter-Varsity Press, 1981), pp. 53–4.

56. E. Hobsbawm, *Interesting Times: A Twentieth-Century Life* (London: Penguin, 2002), p. 6.

57. C. Gearty, 'What is Terror?', in Gearty (ed.), *Terrorism*, p. 495.

58. Guelke, *Age of Terrorism and the International Political System*, p. 7.

59. L. O'Flaherty, 'The Terrorist' (1926), in *Irish Portraits* (London: Sphere, 1970).

60. P. O'Donnell, *The Gates Flew Open* (London: Jonathan Cape, 1932), pp. 75, 178.

61. M. R. Habeck, *Knowing the Enemy: Jihadist Ideology and the War on Terror* (New Haven: Yale University Press, 2006), p. 102. Cf. C. C. Harmon, *Terrorism Today* (London: Routledge, 2008; 1st edn. 2000), p. 2.

62. Osama bin Laden, quoted in Juergensmeyer, *Terror in the Mind of God*, p. 179.

63. Whittaker (ed.), *Terrorism Reader*, p. 7.

64. Marian Price, interviewed by the author, quoted in the *Independent on Sunday*, 2 March 2003.

65. Gearty, 'Introduction', in Gearty (ed.), *Terrorism*, p. xiv.

66. For studies which acknowledge the impossibility of producing finally agreed theories of 'nationalism' and 'revolution' respectively, but which nevertheless offer analysis on the basis of precise definition of the relevant terms, see R. English, *Irish Freedom: The History of Nationalism in Ireland* (London: Pan Macmillan, 2007; 1st edn. 2006), and J. Goodwin, *No Other Way Out: States and Revolutionary Movements, 1945–1991* (Cambridge: Cambridge University Press, 2001).

67. Guelke, *Age of Terrorism and the International Political System*, p. 51.

68. Ludwig Wittgenstein, quoted in R. Monk, *Ludwig Wittgenstein: The Duty of Genius* (London: Jonathan Cape, 1990), p. 338.

69. For example, Charles Townshend's superb edited collection, *The Oxford Illustrated History of Modern War* (Oxford: Oxford University Press, 1997), has only three index references to terrorism.

70. R. Clutterbuck, *Guerrillas and Terrorists* (Athens, Ohio: Ohio University Press, 1980; 1st edn. 1977), p. 11; P. Gilbert, *Terrorism, Security and Nationality: An Introductory Study in Applied Political Philosophy* (London: Routledge, 1994), p. 159; W. R. Mead, *Power, Terror, Peace, and War: America's Grand Strategy in a World at Risk* (New York: Alfred A. Knopf, 2005), p. 167.

71. C. Townshend, *Terrorism* (Oxford: Oxford University Press, 2002), p. 7.

72. R. Jackson, *Writing the War on Terrorism: Language, Politics, and Counter-Terrorism* (Manchester: Manchester University Press, 2005), p. 38.

73. Richardson, *What Terrorists Want*, p. 211.

74. See, e.g., Juergensmeyer, *Terror in the Mind of God*, pp. 75–6.

75. Hoffman, *Inside Terrorism*, p. 14. Cf. 'Terrorism is always political, even when it also evinces other motives, such as the religious, the economic,

or the social' (Harmon, *Terrorism Today*, p. 7). Cf. also Whittaker (ed.), *Terrorism Reader*, p. 9.

76. Harmon, *Terrorism Today*, p. 160.

77. M. Crenshaw, 'Reflections on the Effects of Terrorism', in M. Crenshaw (ed.), *Terrorism, Legitimacy, and Power: The Consequences of Political Violence* (Middletown, Conn.: Wesleyan University Press, 1983), p. 25.

78. The actors can be state as well as non-state, although it makes most sense to study these different categories of terrorism separately. Such an approach does not assume moral equivalence between state and non-state violence; but nor does it rule out the possibility that the condemnation of terrorizing violence might be as appropriate to state action as to that of non-state actors. On the wide variety of groups to have deployed terrorism, see Combs, *Terrorism in the Twenty-First Century*, p. 7.

79. 'The intent of terrorist violence is psychological and symbolic, not material' (Crenshaw, 'Reflections on the Effects of Terrorism', p. 2).

80. J. Conrad, *Under Western Eyes* (Harmondsworth: Penguin, 1957; 1st edn. 1911), p. 24.

81. Harmon, *Terrorism Today*, p. 55.

82. Ibid., p. 46.

CHAPTER 2

1. For an extraordinarily powerful and moving account of this episode and its complex and intimate background (including the falsity of the allegation against the victim), see J. Zulaika, *Basque Violence: Metaphor and Sacrament* (Reno, Nev.: University of Nevada Press, 1988), pp. 74–101.

2. M. Bloom, *Dying to Kill: The Allure of Suicide Terror* (New York: Columbia University Press, 2005), p. 76; M. Chandler and R. Gunaratna, *Countering Terrorism: Can We Meet the Threat of Global Violence?* (London: Reaktion Books, 2007), p. 36.

3. Gilbert, *Terrorism, Security and Nationality*, p. 5; W. Reich (ed.), *Origins of Terrorism: Psychologies, Ideologies, Theologies, States of Mind* (Cambridge: Cambridge University Press, 1990), pp. 27, 60, 78; Pape, *Dying to Win*, p. 23.

4. Horgan, *Psychology of Terrorism*, pp. 50, 75–6; cf. also pp. 53, 62–5.

5. Richardson, *What Terrorists Want*, p. 32 cf. pp. 61, 148–9. Cf. also Whittaker (ed.), *Terrorism Reader*, p. 22, and A. Silke (ed.), *Terrorists, Victims, and Society: Psychological Perspectives on Terrorism and its Consequences* (Chichester: Wiley, 2003), pp. xviii, 6–7, 16–17, 23.

6. Though I myself am unpersuaded by psychoanalytic approaches to the explanation of political violence, it might also be noted that there have been brave attempts to explain violent political conflict in terms of the unconscious. For one such (Lacanian) reading, see A. Millar, *Socio-Ideological Fantasy and the Northern Ireland Conflict: The Other Side* (Manchester: Manchester University Press, 2006).

7. J. Conrad, *The Secret Agent* (Harmondsworth: Penguin, 1963; 1st edn. 1907), p. 73. In Terry Eagleton's rather impish depiction, Conrad's book was 'The first suicide-bomber novel of English literature' (T. Eagleton, *Holy Terror* (Oxford: Oxford University Press, 2005), p. 121).

8. D. K. Gupta, *Understanding Terrorism and Political Violence: The Life Cycle of Birth, Growth, Transformation, and Demise* (London: Routledge, 2008), p. xvii; Pape, *Dying to Win*, p. vi; Juergensmeyer, *Terror in the Mind of God*, pp. 187, 209, 241; Guelke, *Age of Terrorism and the International Political System*, p. 6; Habeck, *Knowing the Enemy*, pp. 122–3; English, *Armed Struggle*, pp. 120–1, 378.

9. And some scholars have begun to put forward innovative, powerful suggestions about how the study of psychology might valuably frame responses to terrorism: M. Taylor and J. Horgan, 'A Conceptual Framework for Addressing Psychological Process in the Development of the Terrorist', *Terrorism and Political Violence*, 18/4 (2006).

10. Richardson, *What Terrorists Want*, p. 113.

11. S. P. Huntington, 'The Clash of Civilizations?', *Foreign Affairs*, 72/3 (Summer 1993); idem, *The Clash of Civilizations and the Remaking of World Order* (London: Touchstone, 1998; 1st edn. 1997); F. Fukuyama, 'The End of History?', *The National Interest*, 16 (1989); idem, *The End of History and the Last Man* (New York: Free Press, 1992).

12. Huntington, *Clash of Civilizations and the Remaking of World Order*, p. 28.

13. Huntington, 'Clash of Civilizations?', pp. 22, 29.

14. R. Scruton, *The West and the Rest: Globalization and the Terrorist Threat* (London: Continuum, 2002), p. vii.

15. Huntington, *Clash of Civilizations and the Remaking of World Order*, pp. 20, 41; see also idem, 'Clash of Civilizations?', p. 24.

16. Scruton, *West and the Rest*, p. 7.

17. M. Ruthven, *A Fury for God: The Islamist Attack on America* (London: Granta, 2002), p. xi.

18. C. Watson, *Modern Basque History: Eighteenth Century to the Present* (Reno, Nev.: Center for Basque Studies, 2003); idem, *Basque Nationalism and Political Violence: The Ideological and Intellectual Origins of ETA* (Reno, Nev.: Center for Basque Studies, 2007).

19. J. Updike, *Terrorist* (London: Hamish Hamilton, 2006), p. 234; see also M. Hamid, *The Reluctant Fundamentalist* (Orlando, Fla.: Harcourt, 2007).

20. See, e.g., the thoughtful treatment in Ruthven, *Fury for God*.

21. I have argued elsewhere that stark resolution of his own particular Irish-British cultural ambiguity helps to explain IRA man Ernie O'Malley's adoption of militant Irish republicanism: R. English, *Ernie O'Malley: IRA Intellectual* (Oxford: Oxford University Press, 1999; 1st edn. 1998).

22. S. M. Hersh, *Chain of Command: The Road from 9/11 to Abu Ghraib* (New York: HarperCollins, 2004), pp. 112–13; Fukuyama, *After the Neocons*, pp. 73–4.

23. Juergensmeyer, *Terror in the Mind of God*, p. xi.

24. Ruthven, *Fury for God*, p. 275.

25. R. Dawkins, *The God Delusion* (London: Black Swan, 2007; 1st edn. 2006), pp. 23, 132, 343, 346, 348. Dawkins's arguments have attracted much criticism in some quarters, not least for the caricatured picture of religion which he is now accused of putting forward; see, e.g., A. McGrath and J. C. McGrath, *The Dawkins Delusion: Atheist Fundamentalism and the Denial of the Divine* (London: SPCK, 2007). But others too have presented the Islamist threat as primarily religious in character, among them M. Phillips, *Londonistan: How Britain is Creating a Terror State Within* (London: Gibson Square, 2006), pp. 274–5.

26. English, *Armed Struggle*, pp. 130–1, 210–11, 371–2.

27. On the historical evolution of Irish republican nationalism, and its association with Catholic identity and grievance, see English, *Irish Freedom*.

28. Bloom, *Dying to Kill*, p. 4.

29. D. Hempton, *Methodism: Empire of the Spirit* (New Haven: Yale University Press, 2005); D. W. Bebbington, *Evangelicalism in Modern Britain: A History from the 1730s to the 1980s* (London: Unwin Hyman, 1989).

30. A. Guelke, *Terrorism and Global Disorder: Political Violence in the Contemporary World* (London: I. B. Tauris, 2006), p. 112.

31. Quoted in F. Halliday, *Two Hours that Shook the World: September 11, 2001: Causes and Consequences* (London: Saqi Books, 2002), p. 233.

32. Habeck, *Knowing the Enemy*, p. 2.

33. M. Ruthven, *Fundamentalism: The Search for Meaning* (Oxford: Oxford University Press, 2004), p. 4.

34. The specifically religious identity of some victims (as with the killing, for example, of Jewish religious students in Jerusalem in March 2008 (*Daily Telegraph*, 7 March 2008)), also lends weight to the religious element involved in terrorist conflict.

35. For a valuable discussion of jihadist thinking, see Habeck, *Knowing the Enemy*.

36. Ibid., p. 53.

37. J. L. Esposito, *Unholy War: Terror in the Name of Islam* (Oxford: Oxford University Press, 2002), pp. 27, 64.

38. B. Lewis, *The Crisis of Islam: Holy War and Unholy Terror* (New York: Modern Library, 2003), p. 137.

39. Juergensmeyer, *Terror in the Mind of God*, pp. 165–71; English, *Armed Struggle*, pp. 210–11.

40. Wilkinson, *Terrorism Versus Democracy*, p. 59.

41. Lewis, *Crisis of Islam*, p. 25.

42. Karl Barth, quoted in T. J. Gorringe, *Karl Barth: Against Hegemony* (Oxford: Oxford University Press, 1999), p. 16.

43. Ruthven, *Fury for God*, p. 38. See also Lewis, *Crisis of Islam*.

44. Juergensmeyer, *Terror in the Mind of God*, p. 70.

45. Ruthven, *Fury for God*, p. 101.

46. Versions of such a theocratic approach can, of course, also be found in other major religions (W. P. Stephens, *Zwingli: An Introduction to his Thought* (Oxford: Oxford University Press, 1994; 1st edn. 1992)).

47. Scruton, *West and the Rest*, p. 65.

48. Pape, *Dying to Win*, pp. 16–17; Bloom, *Dying to Kill*, p. 2.

49. A. R. Norton, *Hezbollah: A Short History* (Princeton: Princeton University Press, 2007).

50. Osama Bin Laden, quoted in Ruthven, *Fury for God*, p. 200. There are those who have disputed whether this account from bin Laden is quite accurate (Wright, *Looming Tower*, p. 94), but there is no doubt about the importance of the Afghan–Soviet conflict for his career.

51. See, e.g., Juergensmeyer, *Terror in the Mind of God*, p. 123.

52. M. Crenshaw, 'The Logic of Terrorism: Terrorist Behaviour as a Product of Strategic Choice', in Reich (ed.), *Origins of Terrorism*, p. 7.

53. See, e.g., Habeck, *Knowing the Enemy*, p. 136.

54. Quoted in Richardson, *What Terrorists Want*, p. 71.

55. Patrick Magee, interviewed by the author, Belfast, 5 March 2002.

56. Alex Maskey, quoted in B. McCaffrey, *Alex Maskey: Man and Mayor* (Belfast: Brehon Press, 2003), p. 217.

57. English, *Irish Freedom*, pp. 382–3.

58. Osama bin Laden, quoted in Kydd and Walter, 'Strategies of Terrorism', p. 63.

59. Pape, *Dying to Win*, p. vi.

60. Bloom, *Dying to Kill*, pp. 1, 79, 83.

61. 'Suicide terrorism in Iraq is driven not by religion, but by a clear stra-
    tegic objective: to prevent the establishment of a government under
    the control of the United States. To do this, the terrorists are attacking
    targets that they hope would undermine the confidence of the Iraq
    population in the Iraqi government's ability to maintain order, and
    especially to discourage Kurds and Sunni from cooperating with the
    government' (Pape, *Dying to Win*, pp. ix, 21).

62. Ruthven, *Fury for God*, p. 28.

63. Eagleton, *Holy Terror*, p. 113.

64. Ayman al-Zawahiri, quoted in Gupta, *Understanding Terrorism and Polit-
    ical Violence*, p. 83.

65. English, *Armed Struggle*, pp. 17–19, 122–3, 139–43.

66. Guelke, *Age of Terrorism and the International Political System*, p. 190.

67. The importance of this distinction is central to the argument of Guelke,
    Terrorism and Global Disorder.

68. Dipak Gupta is very good on this point: *Understanding Terrorism and
    Political Violence*, pp. 197–9.

69. See, for valuable studies of one such example, Zulaika, *Basque Violence*,
    and Watson, *Basque Nationalism and Political Violence*.

70. Richardson, *What Terrorists Want*, p. 24.

71. M. Juergensmeyer, *Global Rebellion: Religious Challenges to the Secular
    State, from Christian Militias to al-Qaeda* (Berkeley: University of Cali-
    fornia Press, 2008), p. 41.

72. For my own explanation, see English, *Irish Freedom*, esp. pp. 11–21,
    431–506.

73. Pape, *Dying to Win*, pp. xiii, 22.

74. L. Colley, *Captives: Britain, Empire and the World 1600–1850* (London:
    Pimlico, 2003; 1st edn. 2002).

75. J. Hutchinson and A. D. Smith (eds.), *Ethnicity* (Oxford: Oxford Uni-
    versity Press, 1996).

76. Huntington, *Clash of Civilizations and the Remaking of World Order*,
    pp. 198–201.

77. Gupta, 'Exploring Roots of Terrorism', in Bjorgo (ed.), *Root Causes
    of Terrorism*, p. 25.

78. Patrick Magee, interviewed by the author, quoted in the *Independent on
    Sunday*, 2 March 2003.

CHAPTER 3

1. *Independent*, 8 July 2005.

2. *Daily Telegraph*, 8 July 2005.

3. IRA Statement, 28 July 2005, copy in author's possession.
4. Clutterbuck, *Guerrillas and Terrorists*, p. 11.
5. A. Roberts, 'The "War on Terror" in Historical Perspective', *Survival*, 47/2 (Summer 2005), p. 104.
6. The literature on the Provisional IRA is extensive. For a variety of interpretations, see English, *Armed Struggle*; Moloney, *Secret History of the IRA*; H. Patterson, *The Politics of Illusion: A Political History of the IRA* (London: Serif, 1997; 1st edn. 1989); R. Alonso, *The IRA and Armed Struggle* (London: Routledge, 2007); M. O'Doherty, *The Trouble with Guns: Republican Strategy and the Provisional IRA* (Belfast: Blackstaff Press, 1998); M. L. R. Smith, *Fighting for Ireland? The Military Strategy of the Irish Republican Movement* (London: Routledge, 1997; 1st edn. 1995); P. Bishop and E. Mallie, *The Provisional IRA* (London: Corgi, 1988; 1st edn. 1987); T. P. Coogan, *The IRA* (London: Fontana, 1987; 1st edn. 1970); K. Toolis, *Rebel Hearts: Journeys within the IRA's Soul* (London: Picador, 1995); P. Taylor, *Provos: The IRA and Sinn Féin* (London: Bloomsbury, 1997).
7. For an extensive elaboration of my own interpretation of how nationalism is best understood, and how it has evolved through Irish history, see English, *Irish Freedom*.
8. The IRA's *Green Book* (a manual apparently begun in 1974, completed in 1978, and produced in 1979), quoted in English, *Armed Struggle*, pp. 213–14.
9. *An Phoblacht/Republican News*, 27 Feb. 1992.
10. IRA General Headquarters Staff representative, quoted in *An Phoblacht/Republican News*, 14 Oct. 1993.
11. *An Phoblacht/Republican News*, 27 March 1997.
12. On loyalist paramilitaries, see the valuable treatments in the following: S. Bruce, *The Red Hand: Protestant Paramilitaries in Northern Ireland* (Oxford: Oxford University Press, 1992); I. S. Wood, *Crimes of Loyalty: A History of the UDA* (Edinburgh: Edinburgh University Press, 2006); J. Cusack and H. McDonald, *UVF* (Dublin: Poolbeg Press, 2000; 1st edn. 1997); *idem*, *UDA: Inside the Heart of Loyalist Terror* (Dublin: Penguin, 2004).
13. *Republican News*, May 1971.
14. IRA Statement (2 Oct. 1979), quoted in *An Phoblacht/Republican News*, 6 Oct. 1979.
15. For valuable reflections on the long-rooted nature of the origins of the conflict, see C. Townshend, *Ireland: The Twentieth Century* (London: Arnold, 1999), and P. Arthur and B. O'Leary, 'Introduction', in J. McGarry and B. O'Leary (eds.), *The Future of Northern Ireland* (Oxford: Oxford University Press, 1990).

16. Brooklyn gun-runner for the Provisionals, George Harrison, speaking of 1970: interviewed by the author, New York, 30 Oct. 2000.

17. Ex-IRA member, interviewed by the author, Belfast, 31 Oct. 2001.

18. Ex-IRA member Anthony McIntyre, interviewed by the author, Belfast, 23 Aug. 2000.

19. Ex-IRA member Marian Price, interviewed by the author, Belfast, 28 Feb. 2002.

20. Ruairí Ó Brádaigh, 'What is Irish Republicanism?' (1970), LHLPC, Sinn Féin (Provisional) Box 1.

21. Patrick Magee, quoted in *Guardian*, 10 Dec. 2001.

22. Pat McGeown, quoted in L. Clarke, *Broadening the Battlefield: The H-Blocks and the Rise of Sinn Féin* (Dublin: Gill and Macmillan, 1987), p. 16.

23. Quoted in *Irish Press*, 2 June 1971.

24. Ex-IRA member Tommy McKearney, interviewed by the author, Belfast, 20 Sept. 2000.

25. Piece by R. G. McAuley, Long Kesh prison, 14 March 1977, LHLPC.

26. *An Phoblacht/Republican News*, 24 May 1980.

27. Gerry Adams, Presidential Address to Sinn Féin's January 1989 *ard fheis*, *An Phoblacht/Republican News*, 2 Feb. 1989.

28. IRA spokesperson, quoted in *An Phoblacht/Republican News*, 17 Aug. 1989.

29. Danny Morrison, quoted in R. W. White, *Provisional Irish Republicans: An Oral and Interpretive History* (Westport, Conn.: Greenwood Press, 1993), p. 173.

30. *An Phoblacht/Republican News*, 14 Feb. 1981.

31. For systematic consideration of the extent to which the IRA achieved its goals, see English, *Armed Struggle*, pp. 338–76, and *idem*, *Irish Freedom*, pp. 398–420.

32. For the contingencies involved in the IRA's emergence and the birth of the Northern Ireland Troubles, see English, *Armed Struggle*, pp. 145–6.

33. M. Kurlansky, *Non-Violence: The History of a Dangerous Idea* (London: Jonathan Cape, 2006), p. 184.

34. G. Adams, *The Politics of Irish Freedom* (Dingle: Brandon, 1986), p. 55.

35. *An Phoblacht/Republican News*, 14 Jan. 1993, 9 Sept. 1993.

36. See Cusack and McDonald, *UVF*.

37. See the outstanding treatment of this theme in P. Hart, *The IRA and its Enemies: Violence and Community in Cork, 1916–1923* (Oxford: Oxford University Press, 1998).

38. R. O'Rawe, *Blanketmen: An Untold Story of the H-Block Hunger Strike* (Dublin: New Island, 2005), pp. 52, 58.

39. Ex-IRA prisoner Anthony McIntyre, interviewed by the author, Belfast, 23 Aug. 2000.

40. See the gripping treatment of this organization in J. Holland and H. McDonald, *INLA: Deadly Divisions* (Dublin: Torc, 1994).

41. *Republican News*, 22 Dec. 1973.

42. *Republicans News*, 7 Feb. 1976.

43. English, *Armed Struggle*, pp. 162–3.

44. *Republican News*, 3 Jan. 1976.

45. Gerry Adams (speaking on 17 June 1979), quoted in *An Phoblacht/Republican News*, 23 June 1979.

46. English, *Irish Freedom*, pp. 382–3. There were precedents for such trends in earlier Irish republican history too: even a celebrated IRA zealot such as Ernie O'Malley (1897–1957) acknowledged that a 'good number' of Irish nationalists in his revolutionary period had reservations about IRA violence (English, *Armed Struggle*, p. 27).

47. G. Adams, *Free Ireland: Towards a Lasting Peace* (Dingle: Brandon, 1995; 1st edn. 1986), p. 191.

48. Adams, *Politics of Irish Freedom*, p. 58.

49. D. Morrison, *Then the Walls Came Down: A Prison Journal* (Cork: Mercier Press, 1999), p. 71.

50. Quoted in J. Holland and S. Phoenix, *Phoenix: Policing the Shadows* (London: Coronet, 1997; 1st edn. 1996), p. 295.

51. Danny Morrison, interviewed by the author, Belfast, 26 May 2000.

52. Tom Hartley, interviewed by the author, Belfast, 24 Oct. 2001.

53. Martin McGuinness, quoted in *Observer*, 6 Feb. 2000.

54. My conviction that the decisive elements producing and sustaining the Northern Ireland Peace Process were local, rather than international, has been reinforced by Eamonn O'Kane's fine essay ('The Impact of Third-Party Intervention on Peace Processes: Northern Ireland and Sri Lanka') in A. Edwards and S. Bloomer (eds.), *Transforming the Peace Process in Northern Ireland: From Terrorism to Democratic Politics* (Dublin: Irish Academic Press, 2008).

55. P. Bew, *The Making and Remaking of the Good Friday Agreement* (Dublin: Liffey Press, 2007), p. 6.

56. M. Mowlam, *Momentum: The Struggle for Peace, Politics, and the People* (London: Hodder & Stoughton, 2002), p. 148.

57. S. O'Callaghan, *The Informer* (London: Bantam, 1998); E. Collins, *Killing Rage* (London: Granta, 1997); M. McGartland, *Fifty Dead Men Walking* (London: Blake, 1998; 1st edn. 1997); Holland and Phoenix, *Phoenix*; M. Ingram and G. Harkin, *Stakeknife: Britain's Secret Agents in Ireland* (Dublin: O'Brien Press, 2004).

58. G. K. Chesterton, *The Man Who Was Thursday: A Nightmare* (Ware: Wordsworth, 1995; 1st edn. 1908), quotations at pp. 116, 118.

59. G. McGladdery, *The Provisional IRA in England: The Bombing Campaign 1973–1997* (Dublin: Irish Academic Press, 2006), p. 5.

60. Tom Hartley, interviewed by the author, Belfast, 24 Oct. 2001.

61. Danny Morrison, interviewed by the author, Belfast, 26 May 2000.

62. For a fuller assessment of the thinking behind the IRA's shift towards Peace Process politics, see English, *Armed Struggle*, pp. 303–15.

63. Powell, *Great Hatred, Little Room*, p. 1.

64. The role of Michael Collins in the violent phase of the pre-independence Irish republican struggle is impressively studied in P. Hart, *Mick: The Real Michael Collins* (London: Pan Macmillan, 2005).

65. Gerry Adams, quoted in *An Phoblacht/Republican News*, 17 Nov. 1983.

66. For thoughtful analyses, see Alonso, *IRA and Armed Struggle*, and B. O'Leary, 'Mission Accomplished? Looking Back at the IRA', *Field Day Review*, 1 (2005).

67. Adams, *Politics of Irish Freedom*, p. 53.

68. 'In fact the defenders [the IRA] brought down more trouble on the people they claimed to be protecting' (Townshend, *Ireland*, p. 208).

69. *An Phoblacht/Republican News*, 31 Dec. 1992.

70. IRA spokesman, quoted in *An Phoblacht/Republican News*, 5 Sept. 1981.

71. G. Murray and J. Tonge, *Sinn Féin and the SDLP: From Alienation to Participation* (Dublin: O'Brien Press, 2005), p. 204. Only 56 per cent of the Catholic community of Northern Ireland currently state a preference that the long-term policy for the region should be unity with the rest of Ireland (*Irish Political Studies Data Yearbook 2008*, p. 189).

72. M. McGuinness, *Bodenstown '86* (London: Wolfe Tone Society, n.d.), p. 10.

73. *Republican News*, 19 May 1973.

74. 'Most local terrorist organizations around the world have a distinctly local agenda' (Haubrich, 'Modern Politics in an Age of Global Terrorism', p. 406).

75. For recent validation of this point, see *Guardian*, 25 July 2006.

76. The Basque country—Euskal Herria, in Basque—comprises territory divided between the Spanish and French states. On the French side of the border lies Iparralde; on the Spanish, Hegoalde.

77. Zulaika, *Basque Violence*, p. 100.

78. Mead, *Power, Terror, Peace, and War*, pp. 3–4.

79. T. H. Johnson, 'Financing Afghan Terrorism: Thugs, Drugs, and Creative Movements of Money', in Giraldo and Trinkunas (eds.), *Terrorism Financing and State Responses*, p. 105.

80. M. Amis, *The Second Plane, September 11: 2001–2007* (London: Jonathan Cape, 2008), p. 21.

81. Halliday, *Two Hours that Shook the World*, p. 31; cf. Gunaratna, *Inside Al-Qaeda*, p. 221.

82. R. A. Clarke, *Against All Enemies: Inside America's War on Terror* (London: Simon & Schuster, 2004), p. 227.

83. Juergensmeyer, *Terror in the Mind of God*, pp. 178–9.

84. There were more than fifty hijackings of civilian airliners each year during 1969, 1970, 1971, 1972 (Guelke, *Terrorism and Global Disorder*, p. 8).

85. Madeleine Albright, quoted in Juergensmeyer, *Terror in the Mind of God*, p. 229.

86. Indeed, hostility towards an occupying force or power has very frequently been crucial to the stimulation of terrorist violence (Cronin, *Ending Terrorism*, p. 13).

87. Amis, *Second Plane*, p. 144. Osama bin Laden was the seventeenth son of the wealthy construction businessman Mohammed bin Laden, who (officially) fathered fifty-four children (Wright, *Looming Tower*, pp. 71–2).

88. Osama bin laden, quoted in Goodwin, 'Theory of Categorical Terrorism', p. 2043.

89. Halliday, *Two Hours that Shook the World*, p. 49.

90. J. Conrad, 'Author's Note' (1920) to *Under Western Eyes*, pp. 8–9.

91. See, e.g., the excellent study by Goodwin, *No Other Way Out*.

92. Quoted in Jackson, *Writing the War on Terrorism*, pp. 10, 191, 194.

93. E. Hobsbawm, *Globalization, Democracy and Terrorism* (London: Little, Brown, 2007), p. 41.

94. B. Riedel, 'Al-Qaeda Strikes Back', *Foreign Affairs*, 86/3 (May/June 2007), p. 29.

95. Much-needed Arabic-speaking members of Special Forces, for example, were moved from Afghanistan to Iraq.

96. C. Campbell and I. Connolly, 'Making War on Terror? Global Lessons from Northern Ireland', *Modern Law Review*, 69/6 (2006), p. 941.

97. E. Foner, *Who Owns History? Rethinking the Past in a Changing World* (New York: Hill and Wang, 2003; 1st edn. 2002), p. 58.

98. Hersh, *Chain of Command*, pp. 188, 229.

99. On the alleged abuses there, see ibid. On the use of torture by the USA in its War on Terror, see G. Monbiot, 'Routine and Systematic Torture is at the Heart of America's War on Terror', *Guardian*, 12 Dec. 2006.

100. A. Roberts, 'Torture and Incompetence in the "War on Terror"', *Survival*, 49/1 (Spring 2007), p. 200.

101. R. Bonner, 'Forever Guantánamo', *New York Review of Books*, 17 April 2008.

102. On which, see Hersh, *Chain of Command*.

103. Campbell and Connolly, 'Making War on Terror?'.

104. Jackson, *Writing the War on Terrorism*, pp. 185, 188.

105. *Guardian*, 1 May 2007.

106. Chandler and Gunaratna, *Countering Terrorism*, pp. 55, 69.

107. Roberts, 'Torture and Incompetence in the "War on Terror"', p. 200.

108. Richardson, *What Terrorists Want*, p. 235.

109. Allison, *Nuclear Terrorism*, p. 136.

110. Hobsbawm, *Globalization, Democracy and Terrorism*, p. 10.

111. In 2007 78 per cent of Iraqis appear to have been opposed to the presence of US forces, 51 per cent of them seeming to think that violence against those forces was acceptable (P. Cockburn, *The Occupation: War and Resistance in Iraq* (London: Verso, 2007; 1st edn. 2006), pp. xiii, xvii).

112. Clarke, *Against All Enemies*, pp. ix–x, 246–7.

113. Richardson, *What Terrorists Want*, p. 10.

114. Riedel, 'Al-Qaeda Strikes Back', p. 24.

115. A. A. Allawi, *The Occupation of Iraq: Winning the War, Losing the Peace* (New Haven: Yale University Press, 2007), pp. xi–xii.

116. *Daily Telegraph*, 1 Sept. 2007. Some British Army soldiers fighting in Iraq have themselves been prominent in publicly condemning the war there, despite their loyalty to the Army as such: 'Blokes are dying for no cause at all and blokes are getting injured for no cause at all'; 'Basra is lost, they are in control now. It's a full-scale riot and the government are just trying to save face … It's a lost battle. We should pull out and call it quits' (Corporal Richard Bradley and Private Paul Barton, quoted in *Independent*, 27 April 2007).

117. Allawi, *Occupation of Iraq*, p. 15; Mead, *Power, Terror, Peace, and War*, p. 151.

118. Pape, *Dying to Win*, pp. v–vi.

119. *Observer*, 12 Nov. 2006.

120. Eliza Manningham-Buller, quoted in 'MI5: 30 Terror Plots Being Planned in UK', *Guardian*, 10 Nov. 2006.

121. Juergensmeyer, *Global Rebellion*, p. 250.

122. D. Byman, *Deadly Connections: States that Sponsor Terrorism* (Cambridge: Cambridge University Press, 2005), pp. 1, 21.

123. Combs, *Terrorism in the Twenty-First Century*, p. 30.

124. D. Byman, 'Passive Sponsors of Terrorism', *Survival*, 47/4 (Winter 2005–6), p. 117.

125. Harmon, *Terrorism Today*, p. 172. Cf 'All terrorist campaigns end' (Cronin, *Ending Terrorism*, p. 7); see also Gupta, *Understanding Terrorism and Political Violence*, pp. 123, 161–80, 183.

126. *Guardian*, 8 May 2007.

127. Quoted in V. S. Pisano, 'The Red Brigades: A Challenge to Italian Democracy', in Gutteridge (ed.), *New Terrorism*, p. 175.

128. Kydd and Walter, 'Strategies of Terrorism', p. 49.

129. A. M. Dershowitz, *Why Terrorism Works: Understanding the Threat, Responding to the Challenge* (New Haven: Yale University Press, 2002), pp. 2, 6.

130. Harmon, *Terrorism Today*, p. 46.

131. Hoffman, *Inside Terrorism*, pp. 64–5.

132. Gearty, *Terror*, p. 2.

133. Wilkinson, *Terrorism Versus Democracy*, pp. 13, 25.

134. M. Abrahms, 'Why Terrorism Does Not Work', *International Security*, 31/2 (Fall 2006), pp. 43–4, 52. Cf. Cronin, *Ending Terrorism*, pp. 35–8.

135. Gupta, *Understanding Terrorism and Political Violence*, pp. 186–91. It is arguable that even the most putatively effective forms of terrorism—those associated with anti-imperial campaigns, overlapping with guerrilla and other forms of struggle—have been less decisive in ending imperial domination than is sometimes assumed (N. Ferguson, *Empire: How Britain Made the Modern World* (London: Penguin, 2004; 1st edn. 2003), pp. 298, 324, 359–60).

136. Dershowitz, *Why Terrorism Works*, pp. 57–78, 88.

137. Burleigh, *Blood and Rage*, p. 84.

138. Ibid., pp. 157–67.

139. Juergensmeyer, *Terror in the Mind of God*, pp. 30–6, 127–8, 133–4.

140. Roberts, '"War on Terror" in Historical Perspective', p. 107.

141. Wilkinson, *Terrorism Versus Democracy*, p. 29.

142. Hasan Nasrallah, quoted in Norton, *Hezbollah*, p. 154.

143. Kurlansky, *Non-Violence*, p. 7.

CHAPTER 4

1. Roberts, 'Torture and Incompetence in the "War on Terror"', p. 199.

2. Hobsbawm, *Globalization, Democracy and Terrorism*, pp. 135, 152–3.

3. *Irish Times*, 8 Oct. 1985.

4. John Adams, *The Death of Klinghoffer* (libretto by Alice Goodman), first performed in 1991; Elektra Nonesuch recording 7559-79281-2.

5. Laqueur, *New Terrorism*, p. 3.

6. J. Buchan, *The Power-House* (Edinburgh: B. and W. Publishing, 1993; 1st edn. 1916).

7. J. Buchan, *Greenmantle* (Harmondsworth: Penguin, 1956; 1st edn. 1916), p. 18.

8. B. Porter, '9/11 ... 1910', *History Today*, 53/11 (Nov. 2003), p. 54.

9. *Daily Telegraph*, 1 July 2007, 3 July 2007.

10. *Daily Telegraph*, 30 June 2007.

11. *Guardian*, 1 May 2007.

12. George W. Bush, 20 Sept. 2001, quoted in Guelke, *Terrorism and Global Disorder*, p. 32.

13. Cf. the shrewd, much earlier observation of Conor Cruise O'Brien that 'The combating of terrorism is not helped by bombastic speeches at high levels, stressing what a monstrous evil terrorism is and that its elimination is to be given the highest priority....Nor does it help to suggest that terrorism is about to be extirpated—because it almost certainly isn't' (C. C. O'Brien, 'Thinking about Terrorism', in *idem, Passion and Cunning and Other Essays* (London: Paladin, 1990; 1st edn. 1988), p. 302).

14. Richardson, *What Terrorists Want*, pp. 10-11.

15. Wilkinson, *Terrorism Versus Democracy*, p. 78. Cf. 'Even strong, stable states such as Britain, Spain, and India have learned to live for long periods at a time with effectively indestructible, if not actually state-threatening, bodies of armed dissidents' (Hobsbawm, *Globalization, Democracy and Terrorism*, p. 37).

16. Whittaker (ed.), *Terrorism Reader*, p. 273.

17. Here, as so often, our practical response to terrorism is unavoidably linked to our definition and explanation of it. Cf. 'Fussing over definitions in such circumstances is anything but pure pedantry. Figuring out what exactly terrorism is and what exactly makes it so wrong is crucial to framing an appropriate response to that evil' (Goodin, *What's Wrong with Terrorism?*, p. 5).

18. Burleigh, *Blood and Rage*, p. ix.

19. Fukuyama, *End of History and the Last Man*, p. 170; cf. pp. 200-1.

20. Dershowitz, *Why Terrorism Works*, pp. 24-5, 85.

21. *Independent*, 9 Feb. 2007.

22. Powell, *Great Hatred, Little Room*, p. 66. Though it is worth also noting the more sceptical attitude of distinguished Northern Ireland civil servant Kenneth Bloomfield regarding the attempted drawing of militant republicans into the democratic political process: K. Bloomfield, *A Tragedy of Errors: The Government and Misgovernment of Northern Ireland*

(Liverpool: Liverpool University Press, 2007), pp. 212–15, 221–6, 245, 249.

23. C. Williams, *Terrorism Explained: The Facts about Terrorism and Terrorist Groups* (Sydney: New Holland Publishers, 2004), p. 111.

24. C. Bell, 'Peace Agreements: Their Nature and Legal Status', *American Journal of International Law*, 100/373 (2006), p. 373.

25. A. Silke, 'Retaliating Against Terrorism', in *idem* (ed.), *Terrorists, Victims, and Society*, p. 230.

26. Cronin, *Ending Terrorism*, p. 8.

27. T. H. Johnson, 'On the Edge of the Big Muddy: The Taliban Resurgence in Afghanistan', *China and Eurasia Forum Quarterly*, 5/2 (2007), pp. 93, 97–8, 100, 119, 122–4.

28. Wilkinson, *Terrorism Versus Democracy*, p. 69.

29. Burleigh, *Blood and Rage*, pp. 114–15.

30. Richardson, *What Terrorists Want*, p. 12.

31. Mike Jackson, in *Daily Telegraph*, 3 Sept. 2007.

32. Dershowitz, *Why Terrorism Works*, p. 2.

33. For a telling recent example from Afghanistan, see the case of Royal Marine Matt Croucher, whose bravery in saving colleagues' lives by throwing himself on to a grenade was reported on the same day as were the growing difficulties of the Afghan military campaign in achieving its objectives (*Daily Telegraph*, 31 March 2008).

34. Quoted in English, *Armed Struggle*, p. 122; cf. D. Morrison, *All the Dead Voices* (Cork: Mercier Press, 2002), pp. 121, 123.

35. Allawi, *Occupation of Iraq*, p. 186.

36. Roberts, ' "War on Terror" in Historical Perspective', p. 109.

37. Wilkinson, *Terrorism Versus Democracy*, p. 95; Cf. M. Sageman, *Understanding Terror Networks* (Philadelphia: University of Pennsylvania Press, 2004), p. 180, and M. Howard, 'What's in a Name? How to Fight Terrorism', *Foreign Affairs*, 81/1 (Jan./Feb. 2002), p. 9.

38. The importance of obtaining high-grade intelligence is reinforced by recognition of the damage done if inaccurate information aggravates disaffection. By the end of September 2005, only 23 of the 895 people arrested under the UK's Terrorism Act of 2000 had actually been convicted of terrorism offences, something which had tended to deepen anger among the Muslim community which was the understandable focus of the authorities' attention (*Guardian*, 12 June 2006).

39. Informers frequently suffer a negative reputation in Irish history. But it is worth remembering—in the Northern Ireland Troubles, for example—how many more people would be dead were it not for the information acquired through agents and informants.

40. *Guardian*, 12 June 2007.
41. Harmon, *Terrorism Today*, pp. 138, 141; cf. Wright, *Looming Tower*, p. 4. Again, we can see the problems caused by the USA having taken its eye off the Afghan ball when the Soviet Union's involvement in that country ended in 1989.
42. Hersh, *Chain of Command*, pp. 59, 73, 76–7, 82, 86, 88, 90, 150–1, 164, 238, 363; Allawi, *Occupation of Iraq*, pp. 7–8.
43. Cockburn, *Occupation*, pp. 11, 34–5.
44. *Guardian*, 9 Jan. 2007.
45. J. R. Faria, 'Terrorist Innovations and Anti-Terrorist Policies', *Terrorism and Political Violence*, 18/1 (2006).
46. *Guardian*, 14 March 2006.
47. B. L. Nacos, Y. Bloch-Elkon, and R. Y. Shapiro, 'Prevention of Terrorism in Post-9/11 America: News Coverage, Public Perceptions, and the Politics of Homeland Security', *Terrorism and Political Violence*, 20/1 (2008).
48. *Observer*, 15 July 2007.
49. *Guardian*, 17 Feb. 2006.
50. There is very good treatment of this in Wright, *Looming Tower*.
51. P. Wilkinson, 'Terrorism versus Liberal Democracy: The Problems of Response', in Gutteridge (ed.), *New Terrorism*, p. 18.
52. A. Danchev, 'Accomplicity: Britain, Torture, and Terror', *British Journal of Politics and International Relations*, 8/4 (Nov. 2006).
53. C. Gearty, *Civil Liberties* (Oxford: Oxford University Press, 2007), quotation at p. 181.
54. Eagleton, *Holy Terror*, pp. 50, 72.
55. Wilkinson, *Terrorism Versus Democracy*, p. 115.
56. R. Dworkin, 'Terror and the Attack on Civil Liberties', *New York Review of Books*, 6 Nov. 2003; C. Gearty, 'It's 1867 All Over Again', *Guardian*, 29 Nov. 2005.
57. M. Cunningham, *British Government Policy in Northern Ireland 1969–2000* (Manchester: Manchester University Press, 2001), pp. 27–8.
58. J. K. Giraldo and H. A. Trinkunas, 'Introduction', in *idem* (eds.), *Terrorism Financing and State Responses*, p. 1.
59. N. Passas, 'Terrorism Financing Mechanisms and Policy Dilemmas', in Giraldo and Trinkunas (eds.), *Terrorism Financing and State Responses*, p. 31.
60. W. Vlcek, 'Development vs. Terrorism: Money Transfers and EU Financial Regulations in the UK', *British Journal of Politics and International Relations*, 10/2 (May 2008).
61. Mockaitis, *'New' Terrorism*, p. 103.

62. Phillips, *Londonistan*, pp. 11–12.
63. C. Townshend, *Making the Peace: Public Order and Public Security in Modern Britain* (Oxford: Oxford University Press, 1993), p. 4.
64. Ferguson *et al.*, *Four Faces of Nuclear Terrorism*, pp. 143, 318.
65. Ibid., pp. 328–9.
66. Byman, 'Passive Sponsors of Terrorism', pp. 138–9.
67. Ferguson *et al.*, *Four Faces of Nuclear Terrorism*, p. 82.
68. *Independent*, 7 March 2007.
69. Ian Paisley, interviewed by the author, Belfast, 21 Feb. 1994.
70. Mead, *Power, Terror, Peace, and War*, p. 147.
71. Cronin is very good on this point: *Ending Terrorism*, pp. 66–72.
72. For a powerful account of the awfulness of 'the reality of what violence does' in terrorist-related conflicts, see K. Myers, *Watching the Door: A Memoir 1971–1978* (Dublin: Lilliput Press, 2006), quotation at p. vii.
73. Wright, *Looming Tower*, p. 8.
74. See, e.g., Burleigh, *Blood and Rage*, p. 126.
75. Danny Morrison, interviewed by the author, quoted in the *Independent on Sunday*, 2 March 2003.
76. M. Crenshaw, 'Conclusions', in *idem* (ed.), *Terrorism, Legitimacy, and Power*, p. 149.

BIBLIOGRAPHY

Abrahms, M., 'Why Terrorism Does Not Work', *International Security*, 31/2 (Fall 2006).

Adams, G., *Free Ireland: Towards a Lasting Peace* (Dingle: Brandon, 1995; 1st edn. 1986).

—— *The Politics of Irish Freedom* (Dingle: Brandon, 1986).

Allawi, A. A., *The Occupation of Iraq: Winning the War, Losing the Peace* (New Haven: Yale University Press, 2007).

Allison, G., *Nuclear Terrorism: The Risks and Consequences of the Ultimate Disaster* (London: Constable, 2006; 1st edn. 2004).

Alonso, R., *The IRA and Armed Struggle* (London: Routledge, 2007).

Amis, M., *The Second Plane, September 11: 2001–2007* (London: Jonathan Cape, 2008).

Barker, J., *The No-Nonsense Guide to Terrorism* (London: Verso, n.d.).

Bebbington, D. W., *Evangelicalism in Modern Britain: A History from the 1730s to the 1980s* (London: Unwin Hyman, 1989).

Bell, C., 'Peace Agreements: Their Nature and Legal Status', *American Journal of International Law*, 100/373 (2006).

Bellamy, A. J., 'Dirty Hands and Lesser Evils in the War on Terror', *British Journal of Politics and International Relations*, 9/3 (August 2007).

Bew, P., *The Making and Remaking of the Good Friday Agreement* (Dublin: Liffey Press, 2007).

Bishop, P., and Mallie, E., *The Provisional IRA* (London: Corgi, 1988; 1st edn. 1987).

Bjorgo, T. (ed.), *Root Causes of Terrorism: Myths, Realities and Ways Forward* (London: Routledge, 2005).

Bloom, M., *Dying to Kill: The Allure of Suicide Terror* (New York: Columbia University Press, 2005).

Bloomfield, K., *Stormont in Crisis: A Memoir* (Belfast: Blackstaff Press, 1994).

—— *A Tragedy of Errors: The Government and Misgovernment of Northern Ireland* (Liverpool: Liverpool University Press, 2007).

Bruce, S., *The Red Hand: Protestant Paramilitaries in Northern Ireland* (Oxford: Oxford University Press, 1992).

—— *Religion in the Modern World: From Cathedrals to Cults* (Oxford: Oxford University Press, 1997; 1st edn. 1996).

Buchan, J., *Greenmantle* (Harmondsworth: Penguin, 1956; 1st edn. 1916).

—— *The Power-House* (Edinburgh: B. and W. Publishing, 1993; 1st edn. 1916).

Burleigh, M., *Blood and Rage: A Cultural History of Terrorism* (London: Harper Press, 2008).

Byman, D., *Deadly Connections: States that Sponsor Terrorism* (Cambridge: Cambridge University Press, 2005).

—— 'Friends Like These: Counterinsurgency and the War on Terrorism', *International Security*, 31/2 (Fall 2006).

—— 'Passive Sponsors of Terrorism', *Survival*, 47/4 (Winter 2005–6).

Campbell, C., ' "Wars on Terror" and Vicarious Hegemons: The UK, International Law, and the Northern Ireland Conflict', *International and Comparative Law Quarterly*, 54 (April 2005).

—— and Connolly, I., 'Making War on Terror? Global Lessons from Northern Ireland', *Modern Law Review*, 69/6 (2006).

Chandler, M., and Gunaratna, R., *Countering Terrorism: Can We Meet the Threat of Global Violence?* (London: Reaktion Books, 2007).

Chesterton, G. K., *The Man Who Was Thursday: A Nightmare* (Ware: Wordsworth, 1995; 1st edn. 1908).

Chomsky, N., *The Culture of Terrorism* (London: Pluto, 1989).

—— *Power and Terror: Post-9/11 Talks and Interviews* (New York: Seven Stories Press, 2003).

Clarke, L., *Broadening the Battlefield: The H-Blocks and the Rise of Sinn Féin* (Dublin: Gill and Macmillan, 1987).

Clarke, R. A., *Against All Enemies: Inside America's War on Terror* (London: Simon & Schuster, 2004).

Clausewitz, C. von, *On War* (Harmondsworth: Penguin, 1968; 1st edn. 1832).

Clutterbuck, R., *Guerrillas and Terrorists* (Athens, Ohio: Ohio University Press, 1980; 1st edn. 1977).

Cockburn, P., *The Occupation: War and Resistance in Iraq* (London: Verso, 2007; 1st edn. 2006).

Colley, L., *Captives: Britain, Empire and the World 1600–1850* (London: Pimlico, 2003; 1st edn. 2002).

Collins, E., *Killing Rage* (London: Granta, 1997).

Combs, C. C., *Terrorism in the Twenty-First Century* (London: Pearson Education, 2003; 1st edn. 1997).

Conrad, J., *The Secret Agent* (Harmondsworth: Penguin, 1963; 1st edn. 1907).

—— *Under Western Eyes* (Harmondsworth: Penguin, 1957; 1st edn. 1911).

Coogan, T. P., *The IRA* (London: Fontana, 1987; 1st edn. 1970).

Crenshaw, M. (ed.), *Terrorism, Legitimacy, and Power: The Consequences of Political Violence* (Middletown, Conn.: Wesleyan University Press, 1983).

Cronin, A. K., *Ending Terrorism: Lessons for Defeating al-Qaeda* (London: Routledge, 2008).

Cunningham, M., *British Government Policy in Northern Ireland 1969–2000* (Manchester: Manchester University Press, 2001).

Cusack, J., and McDonald, H., *UDA: Inside the Heart of Loyalist Terror* (Dublin: Penguin, 2004).

—— *UVF* (Dublin: Poolbeg Press, 2000; 1st edn. 1997).

Danchev, A., 'Accomplicity: Britain, Torture, and Terror', *British Journal of Politics and International Relations*, 8/4 (November 2006).

Dawkins, R., *The God Delusion* (London: Black Swan, 2007; 1st edn. 2006).

de Cataldo Neuburger, L., and Valentini, T., *Women and Terrorism* (Basingstoke: Macmillan, 1996; 1st edn. 1992).

Dershowitz, A. M., *Why Terrorism Works: Understanding the Threat, Responding to the Challenge* (New Haven: Yale University Press, 2002).

Dunleavy, P., and O'Leary, B., *Theories of the State: The Politics of Liberal Democracy* (Basingstoke: Macmillan, 1987).

Eagleton, T., *Holy Terror* (Oxford: Oxford University Press, 2005).

Edwards, A., and Bloomer, S. (eds.), *Transforming the Peace Process in Northern Ireland: From Terrorism to Democratic Politics* (Dublin: Irish Academic Press, 2008).

Elsdon, R., *Bent World: Science, The Bible and the Environment* (Leicester: Inter-Varsity Press, 1981).

English, R., *Armed Struggle: The History of the IRA* (New York: Oxford University Press, 2005; 1st edn. 2003).

—— *Ernie O'Malley: IRA Intellectual* (Oxford: Oxford University Press, 1999; 1st edn. 1998).

—— *Irish Freedom: The History of Nationalism in Ireland* (London: Pan Macmillan, 2007; 1st edn. 2006).

—— and Townshend, C. (eds.), *The State: Historical and Political Dimensions* (London: Routledge, 1999).

Esposito, J. L., *Unholy War: Terror in the Name of Islam* (Oxford: Oxford University Press, 2002).

Faria, J. R., 'Terrorist Innovations and Anti-Terrorist Policies', *Terrorism and Political Violence*, 18/1 (2006).

Ferguson, C. D., Potter, W. C., Sands, A., Spector, L. S., and Wehling, F. L., *The Four Faces of Nuclear Terrorism* (New York: Routledge, 2005).

Ferguson, N., *Empire: How Britain Made the Modern World* (London: Penguin, 2004; 1st edn. 2003).

Foner, E., *Who Owns History? Rethinking the Past in a Changing World* (New York: Hill and Wang, 2003; 1st edn. 2002).

Freedman, L., 'Strategic Terror and Amateur Psychology', *Political Quarterly*, 76/2 (2005).

—— 'The Transatlantic Agenda: Vision and Counter-Vision', *Survival*, 47/4 (Winter 2005–6).

Fukuyama, F., *After the Neocons: America at the Crossroads* (London: Profile Books, 2006).

—— 'The End of History?', *The National Interest*, 16 (1989).

—— *The End of History and the Last Man* (New York: Free Press, 1992).

Gearson, J., 'The Nature of Modern Terrorism', *Political Quarterly*, 73 (August 2002).

Gearty, C., *Can Human Rights Survive?* (Cambridge: Cambridge University Press, 2006).

—— *Civil Liberties* (Oxford: Oxford University Press, 2007).

—— *Terror* (London: Faber & Faber, 1992; 1st edn. 1991).

—— (ed.), *Terrorism* (Aldershot: Dartmouth, 1996).

George, A. (ed.), *Western State Terrorism* (Cambridge: Polity Press, 1991).

Gilbert, P., *Terrorism, Security and Nationality: An Introductory Study in Applied Political Philosophy* (London: Routledge, 1994).

Giraldo, J. K., and Trinkunas, H. A. (eds.), *Terrorism Financing and State Responses: A Comparative Perspective* (Stanford, Calif.: Stanford University Press, 2007).

Goodin, R. E., *What's Wrong with Terrorism?* (Cambridge: Polity Press, 2006).

Goodwin, J., *No Other Way Out: States and Revolutionary Movements, 1945–1991* (Cambridge: Cambridge University Press, 2001).

—— 'A Theory of Categorical Terrorism', *Social Forces*, 84/4 (June 2006).

Gorringe, T. J., *Karl Barth: Against Hegemony* (Oxford: Oxford University Press, 1999).

Guelke, A., *The Age of Terrorism and the International Political System* (London: I. B. Tauris, 1998; 1st edn. 1995).

—— *Terrorism and Global Disorder: Political Violence in the Contemporary World* (London: I. B. Tauris, 2006).

Gunaratna, R., *Inside Al-Qaeda: Global Network of Terror* (London: Hurst, 2002).

Gupta, D. K., *Understanding Terrorism and Political Violence: The Life Cycle of Birth, Growth, Transformation, and Demise* (London: Routledge, 2008).

Gutteridge, W. (ed.), *The New Terrorism* (London: Mansell Publishing, 1986).

Habeck, M. R., *Knowing the Enemy: Jihadist Ideology and the War on Terror* (New Haven: Yale University Press, 2006).

Halliday, F., *Two Hours that Shook the World: September 11, 2001: Causes and Consequences* (London: Saqi Books, 2002).

Hamid, M., *The Reluctant Fundamentalist* (Orlando, Fla.: Harcourt, 2007).

Harmon, C. C., *Terrorism Today* (London: Routledge, 2008; 1st edn. 2000).

Hart, P., *The IRA and its Enemies: Violence and Community in Cork, 1916–1923* (Oxford: Oxford University Press, 1998).

—— *Mick: The Real Michael Collins* (London: Pan Macmillan, 2005).

Haubrich, D., 'Modern Politics in an Age of Global Terrorism: New Challenges for Domestic Public Policy', *Political Studies*, 54/2 (June 2006).

Heiberg, M., O'Leary, B., and Tirman, J. (eds.), *Terror, Insurgency and the State: Ending Protracted Conflicts* (Philadelphia: University of Pennsylvania Press, 2007).

Hempton, D., *Methodism: Empire of the Spirit* (New Haven: Yale University Press, 2005).

Hersh, S. M., *Chain of Command: The Road from 9/11 to Abu Ghraib* (New York: HarperCollins, 2004).

Hobsbawm, E., *Globalization, Democracy and Terrorism* (London: Little, Brown, 2007).

—— *Interesting Times: A Twentieth-Century Life* (London: Penguin, 2002).

Hoffman, B., *Inside Terrorism* (London: Victor Gollancz, 1998).

Holland, J., and McDonald, H., *INLA: Deadly Divisions* (Dublin: Torc, 1994).

—— and Phoenix, S., *Phoenix: Policing the Shadows* (London: Coronet, 1997; 1st edn. 1996).

Horgan, J., *The Psychology of Terrorism* (London: Routledge, 2005).

Howard, M., 'What's in a Name? How to Fight Terrorism', *Foreign Affairs*, 81/1 (January/February 2002).

Huntington, S. P., 'The Clash of Civilizations?', *Foreign Affairs*, 72/3 (Summer 1993).

—— *The Clash of Civilizations and the Remaking of World Order* (London: Touchstone, 1998; 1st edn. 1997).

Hutchinson, J., and Smith, A. D. (eds.), *Ethnicity* (Oxford: Oxford University Press, 1996).

Ingram, M., and Harkin, G., *Stakeknife: Britain's Secret Agents in Ireland* (Dublin: O'Brien Press, 2004).

Jackson, R., *Writing the War on Terrorism: Language, Politics, and Counter-Terrorism* (Manchester: Manchester University Press, 2005).

Johnson, T. H., 'On the Edge of the Big Muddy: The Taliban Resurgence in Afghanistan', *China and Eurasia Forum Quarterly*, 5/2 (2007).

Juergensmeyer, M., *Global Rebellion: Religious Challenges to the Secular State, from Christian Militias to al-Qaeda* (Berkeley: University of California Press, 2008).

Juergensmeyer, M., *Terror in the Mind of God: The Global Rise of Religious Violence* (Berkeley: University of California Press, 2001; 1st edn. 2000).

Kurlansky, M., *Non-Violence: The History of a Dangerous Idea* (London: Jonathan Cape, 2006).

Kuznar, L. A., and Lutz, J. M., 'Risk Sensitivity and Terrorism', *Political Studies*, 55/2 (June 2007).

Kydd, A. H., and Walter, B. F., 'The Strategies of Terrorism', *International Security*, 31/1 (Summer 2006).

Laqueur, W., *The New Terrorism: Fanaticism and the Arms of Mass Destruction* (London: Phoenix Press, 2001; 1st edn. 1999).

Lewis, B., *The Crisis of Islam: Holy War and Unholy Terror* (New York: Modern Library, 2003).

Lodge, J. (ed.), *Terrorism: A Challenge to the State* (Oxford: Martin Robertson, 1981).

McCaffrey, B., *Alex Maskey: Man and Mayor* (Belfast: Brehon Press, 2003).

McGarry, J., and O'Leary, B. (eds.), *The Future of Northern Ireland* (Oxford: Oxford University Press, 1990).

McGartland, M., *Fifty Dead Men Walking* (London: Blake, 1998; 1st edn. 1997).

McGladdery, G., *The Provisional IRA in England: The Bombing Campaign 1973–1997* (Dublin: Irish Academic Press, 2006).

McGrath, A., and McGrath, J. C., *The Dawkins Delusion: Atheist Fundamentalism and the Denial of the Divine* (London: SPCK, 2007).

McGuinness, M., *Bodenstown '86* (London: Wolfe Tone Society, n.d.).

Mead, W. R., *Power, Terror, Peace, and War: America's Grand Strategy in a World at Risk* (New York: Alfred A. Knopf, 2005).

Millar, A., *Socio-Ideological Fantasy and the Northern Ireland Conflict: The Other Side* (Manchester: Manchester University Press, 2006).

Mockaitis, T. R., *The 'New' Terrorism: Myths and Reality* (Westport, Conn.: Praeger Security International, 2007).

Moloney, E., *A Secret History of the IRA* (London: Penguin, 2007; 1st edn. 2002).

Monk, R., *Ludwig Wittgenstein: The Duty of Genius* (London: Jonathan Cape, 1990).

Morrison, D., *All the Dead Voices* (Cork: Mercier Press, 2002).

—— *Then the Walls Came Down: A Prison Journal* (Cork: Mercier Press, 1999).

Mowlam, M., *Momentum: The Struggle for Peace, Politics, and the People* (London: Hodder & Stoughton, 2002).

Murray, G., and Tonge, J., *Sinn Féin and the SDLP: From Alienation to Participation* (Dublin: O'Brien Press, 2005).

Myers, K., *Watching the Door: A Memoir 1971–1978* (Dublin: Lilliput Press, 2006).

Nacos, B. L., Bloch-Elkon, Y., and Shapiro, R. Y., 'Prevention of Terrorism in Post-9/11 America: News Coverage, Public Perceptions, and the Politics of Homeland Security', *Terrorism and Political Violence*, 20/1 (2008).

Norton, A. R., *Hezbollah: A Short History* (Princeton: Princeton University Press, 2007).

O'Brien, C. C., *Passion and Cunning and Other Essays* (London: Paladin, 1990; 1st edn. 1988).

O'Callaghan, S., *The Informer* (London: Bantam, 1998).

O'Doherty, M., *The Trouble with Guns: Republican Strategy and the Provisional IRA* (Belfast: Blackstaff Press, 1998).

O'Donnell, P., *The Gates Flew Open* (London: Jonathan Cape, 1932).

O'Flaherty, L., *Irish Portraits* (London: Sphere, 1970).

O'Leary, B., 'Mission Accomplished? Looking Back at the IRA', *Field Day Review*, 1 (2005).

O'Rawe, R., *Blanketmen: An Untold Story of the H-Block Hunger Strike* (Dublin: New Island, 2005).

Pape, R. A., *Dying to Win: Why Suicide Terrorists Do It* (London: Gibson Square Books, 2006; 1st edn. 2005).

Patterson, H., *The Politics of Illusion: A Political History of the IRA* (London: Serif, 1997; 1st edn. 1989).

Phillips, M., *Londonistan: How Britain is Creating a Terror State Within* (London: Gibson Square, 2006).

Porter, B., '9/11 ... 1910', *History Today*, 53/11 (November 2003).

Powell, J., *Great Hatred, Little Room: Making Peace in Northern Ireland* (London: Bodley Head, 2008).

Primoratz, I., 'The Morality of Terrorism', *Journal of Applied Philosophy*, 14/3 (1997).

Reich, W. (ed.), *Origins of Terrorism: Psychologies, Ideologies, Theologies, States of Mind* (Cambridge: Cambridge University Press, 1990).

Richardson, L., *What Terrorists Want: Understanding the Terrorist Threat* (London: John Murray, 2006).

Riedel, B., 'Al-Qaeda Strikes Back', *Foreign Affairs*, 86/3 (May/June 2007).

Roberts, A., 'Torture and Incompetence in the "War on Terror"', *Survival*, 49/1 (Spring 2007).

——'The "War on Terror" in Historical Perspective', *Survival*, 47/2 (Summer 2005).

Royal Institute of International Affairs, *Terrorism and International Order* (London: Routledge & Kegan Paul, 1986).

Ruthven, M., *Fundamentalism: The Search for Meaning* (Oxford: Oxford University Press, 2004).

—— *A Fury for God: The Islamist Attack on America* (London: Granta, 2002).

Sageman, M., *Understanding Terror Networks* (Philadelphia: University of Pennsylvania Press, 2004).

Scheffler, S., 'Is Terrorism Morally Distinctive?', *Journal of Political Philosophy*, 14/1 (2006).

Schmid, A. P., and Jongman, A. J. (eds.), *Political Terrorism* (Amsterdam: North Holland Publishing, 1988).

Scruton, R., *The West and the Rest: Globalization and the Terrorist Threat* (London: Continuum, 2002).

Silke, A. (ed.), *Terrorists, Victims, and Society: Psychological Perspectives on Terrorism and its Consequences* (Chichester: Wiley, 2003).

Simon, S., and Benjamin, D., 'America and the New Terrorism', *Survival*, 42/1 (Spring 2000).

Smith, M. L. R., *Fighting for Ireland? The Military Strategy of the Irish Republican Movement* (London: Routledge, 1997; 1st edn. 1995).

Stephens, W. P., *Zwingli: An Introduction to his Thought* (Oxford: Oxford University Press, 1994; 1st edn. 1992).

Takeyh, R., 'Iran, Israel, and the Politics of Terrorism', *Survival*, 48/4 (Winter 2006–7).

Taylor, M., and Horgan, J., 'A Conceptual Framework for Addressing Psychological Process in the Development of the Terrorist', *Terrorism and Political Violence*, 18/4 (2006).

Taylor, P., *Provos: The IRA and Sinn Féin* (London: Bloomsbury, 1997).

Toolis, K., *Rebel Hearts: Journeys within the IRA's Soul* (London: Picador, 1995).

Townshend, C., *Ireland: The Twentieth Century* (London: Arnold, 1999).

—— *Making the Peace: Public Order and Public Security in Modern Britain* (Oxford: Oxford University Press, 1993).

—— *Terrorism* (Oxford: Oxford University Press, 2002).

—— (ed.), *The Oxford Illustrated History of Modern War* (Oxford: Oxford University Press, 1997).

Tucker, D., 'What is New about the New Terrorism and How Dangerous is It?', *Terrorism and Political Violence*, 13/3 (2001).

Updike, J., *Terrorist* (London: Hamish Hamilton, 2006).

Vlcek, W., 'Development vs. Terrorism: Money Transfers and EU Financial Regulations in the UK', *British Journal of Politics and International Relations*, 10/2 (May 2008).

Watson, C., *Basque Nationalism and Political Violence: The Ideological and Intellectual Origins of ETA* (Reno, Nev.: Center for Basque Studies, 2007).

——— *Modern Basque History: Eighteenth Century to the Present* (Reno, Nev.: Center for Basque Studies, 2003).

White, R. W., *Provisional Irish Republicans: An Oral and Interpretive History* (Westport, Conn.: Greenwood Press, 1993).

Whittaker, D. J. (ed.), *The Terrorism Reader* (London: Routledge, 2003; 1st edn. 2001).

Wilkinson, P., *Terrorism Versus Democracy: The Liberal State Response* (London: Frank Cass, 2001; 1st edn. 2000).

Williams, C., *Terrorism Explained: The Facts about Terrorism and Terrorist Groups* (Sydney: New Holland Publishers, 2004).

Wood, I. S., *Crimes of Loyalty: A History of the UDA* (Edinburgh: Edinburgh University Press, 2006).

Wright, L., *The Looming Tower: Al-Qaeda's Road to 9/11* (London: Penguin, 2007; 1st edn. 2006).

Zinn, H., *Terrorism and War* (New York: Seven Stories Press, 2002).

Zulaika, J., *Basque Violence: Metaphor and Sacrament* (Reno, Nev.: University of Nevada Press, 1988).

PHOTOGRAPHIC ACKNOWLEDGEMENTS

© Brooks Kraft/Corbis: 4; © Reuters/Corbis: 14; © AP Photo/ Empics: 1, 11; © Daniel Ochoa de Olza/AP Photo/Empics: 6; © AFP/Getty Images: 10; © Getty Images: 2, 7; © Handout/Getty Images: 9, 15; © Time & Life Pictures/Getty Images: 3; © Rex Features: 5, 12; © Bill Rolston: 8; © ullsteinbild/TopFoto.co.uk: 13

INDEX